PCs

in eas

Harshad Kotecha

**COMPUTER
STEP**

In easy steps is an imprint of Computer Step
Southfield Road . Southam
Warwickshire CV47 OFB . England

Tel: 01926 817999 Fax: 01926 817005
http://www.computerstep.com

Fifth edition

Notice of Liability
Every effort has been made to ensure that this book contains accurate
and current information. However, Computer Step and the author shall
not be liable for any loss or damage suffered by readers as a result of
any information contained herein.

Trademarks
All trademarks are acknowledged as belonging to their respective
companies.

Acknowledgement
Computer Step would like to thank Stuart Yarnold for his contribution
to this edition.

Printed and bound in the United Kingdom

ISBN 1-84078-045-2

Contents

3   The Internet   79

4   Software   113

5   Peripherals   141

6   Upgrading   159

7 Troubleshooting 171

Index 189

The PC Unravelled

This chapter covers the history of the personal computer and all its various system components. Hints and tips are given for those about to purchase a PC for the first time.

Covers

Chapter One

Introduction

Many people, having made the decision to buy a PC, are unable to contain their enthusiasm and dive into the first computer shop they can find. A couple of weeks later they will, all too often, regret the choices they have made. Not only that but very often it later becomes apparent that the sales assistant has given them some very iffy advice based on what was in *his* interests rather than theirs.

If they had only waited until understanding something about computers they could have saved themselves a tidy sum. This isn't only due to what they *have* bought but also to do with what they *haven't* bought and then subsequently have to buy as an upgrade at a higher cost than if it had been part of the original system.

One of the intentions of this book is to guide you through the initial buying process, telling you where to buy and where not to buy, what questions to ask and what to look out for when dealing with computer sales-staff.

Another aim of this book is to give you a basic understanding, without bogging you down with too much detail, about what goes on inside your PC. Motherboards, CPUs, Hard Drives, Graphic Cards, RAM memory chips and all the other major components of your system are explained. This knowledge isn't essential to operate your PC but will greatly enhance your enjoyment of computing.

When you have bought your system and got it up and running you are now introduced to the PC's operating system, Windows. This book doesn't devote too much space to the actual mechanics of Windows as it's already an exhaustively covered subject with many books written on the topic, but instead concentrates on its basic operating principles. You'll find a comprehensive help file within Windows itself, which will answer most of your questions.

Internet usage is growing rapidly and once you are connected up, it is very straightforward to use. However making the connection itself is less easy due to the increasing number and different types of Internet Service

Providers. There are also a number of different payment schemes and once again you are guided through the choices so that hopefully you make the one that is right for you. There is also plenty of helpful advice to assist you in getting the best out of the Internet.

Having tried out the software bundled with your PC (usually pretty basic), you'll soon be looking round the software shops to see what's available. There is in fact a vast range of programs out there covering a multitude of applications for you to install on your PC, some of it good, some of it not so good. A wide range of popular applications are evaluated here.

There is a whole host of peripherals on the market that you can add to your new system, ranging from the near indispensable such as printers, storage and backup devices, etc. to highly desirable but non essential items such as scanners, digital cameras, television/teletext tuner cards etc. A comprehensive section of the book is given over to a detailed analysis of everything presently on the market, explaining clearly and concisely, the pros and cons of each.

Given the frightening speed with which PCs become obsolete these days it is an absolute *must* that your chosen system has the capacity to be upgraded. Be warned that many PCs on the market are extremely limited in this respect and by the time you find this out it will be too late. A section of this book is devoted to the procedures necessary for upgrading your PC.

It won't be long before you realise that there is a lot more to your computer than initially meets the eye. They are incredibly complex machines, a fact that is further complicated by all the extras we add on in the form of peripherals. Given this, it's hardly surprising that they tend to go wrong on a fairly regular basis. It's also a fact that many PC problems are caused by the user and so in an effort to help you avoid some of these mistakes, there is a chapter devoted to troubleshooting and user guidelines. This chapter also explains how to maintain your system.

Computers don't require a great deal of maintenance but there are some very important dos and don'ts which some people completely ignore to their eventual cost. Perusal of this chapter will enable the reader to avoid costly phone calls to computer help lines.

Throughout, the book is intended to give clear and concise advice from a buying and operating point of view, based on the author's personal experience with particular regard to helping the reader avoid the many pitfalls and misconceptions associated with PCs.

The Computer Story So Far

Going right back to the beginning it could be argued that the abacus is the earliest link with the modern PC although it would also have to be said that this is a somewhat tenuous link. Nevertheless it was the first mechanical device for performing calculations and in the hands of an expert can still be a match for many modern calculating machines. Thus it deserves a mention.

Skipping forward a few years to the 17th century (the abacus is reckoned to be Babylonian in origin), the first mechanical calculating machine was invented in Germany by Wilhelm Schickard.

In 1642 this was developed further by a Frenchman, Blaise Pascal, who came up with a digital machine employing gears and columns of digits.

The 17th century also saw the invention of punched cards to control data processing, an invention that is still used today (a musical box movement is a typical example).

In 1847 came the significant development of Boolean algebra and the Binary system of mathematics by the Englishman George Boole. The binary code is the basis of today's digital computers.

Moving forward to the 20th century we see the first modern electronic computers employing the use of vacuum tubes or valves. The first electronic computer, although it still employed electo-mechanical devices, was built in America in 1946. Called the ENIAC it was a beast of a machine employing some 18,000 valves and was over 24 metres long. Nevertheless it could perform some 5000 calculations a second.

A major breakthrough in computer development came in the 1960's with the introduction of transistorised circuitry. Due to the minute size of the transistor in comparison with the valve, its reliability and low power consumption, it was now possible to build much smaller machines but with vastly greater capabilities (typically up 100,000 instructions a second).

With the introduction of integrated circuitry, the forerunner of the modern chip, came astounding advances in computer technology. Computers were now getting smaller and smaller, faster and faster, not to mention cheaper.

As the development of integrated circuits continued, the Intel Corporation introduced the first microprocessor chip in 1974 and this was swiftly followed by the first RAM chip, which did away with the need for electro-magnetic memories. This further reduced the size of computers whilst again increasing their capabilities.

By the 1980's chips were being built that contained hundreds of thousands of transistors and associated components. In 1984 IBM launched the IBM 80286, also known as an AT, which offered much improved memory capability enabling several programs to be loaded simultaneously.

In 1986 Compaq brought out an improved version of the AT. This computer introduced the concept of multitasking, whereby the user could run more than one application at the same time.

Today there are hundreds of PC brand names.

This period saw many other manufacturers enter the computer market as the commercial potential of home computers started to become apparent. The resultant increase in competition inevitably saw dramatic falls in prices that further fuelled the demand. In an effort to regain some of the ground it had lost, IBM brought out the PS/2 in 1987 together with a new operating system called OS/2. Unfortunately for IBM, Microsoft were on the scene with Windows 3.1 which proved to be the more popular of the two systems.

1989 saw Intel bring out the 486 chip which doubled or trebled the speed of PCs. In the meantime Microsoft was consolidating its grip on the operating system market.

By 1993 PCs were running as fast as 90Mhz with the introduction of the Pentium chipset but very soon, improved versions saw speeds of up to 200Mhz. These chips rendered the old 486 virtually obsolete and as prices dropped they were taken up by most of the PC manufacturers.

1995 saw the release of Windows 95 which came with a radically overhauled interface introducing a new concept of folder windows and the ability to create shortcuts whereby programs could be started from anywhere chosen by the user. With the introduction of this new operating system, the PC as we know it today was really born. In late 1995 Intel released the Pentium Pro chip that was a further improvement on the original Pentium.

1997 saw the advent of a new technology called MMX (MultiMedia eXtensions) designed to offer better support for the developing concept of multimedia. Later that year Intel brought out the Pentium II, which was designed to integrate with Microsoft's impending Windows 98. Processor speeds were by now up to 300 MHz.

In 1998 Microsoft released Windows 98 with its vastly improved Internet facilities and support for the new technology of Universal Serial BUS (USB).

...cont'd

 Microsoft and Intel dominate the PC market today. About 90 percent of PCs use Intel's processors and Microsoft's operating system software.

During the 1990's development of other computer hardware, particularly hard drives, was equally frenetic. High quality inkjet printers, scanners and digital cameras all came tumbling down in price to the point now where it's almost silly not to have them. Modems also saw rapid development due to the increasing popularity of the Internet.

Recent years have also seen an astonishing growth in the PC games market as the power that PCs now have has enabled the games manufacturers to produce 3-dimensional games of incredible realism. Indeed the development of games technology, in particular that of 3D graphics, could almost be said to be dragging the rest of the PC industry along with it as it attempts to keep up with the technological demands of the games industry.

More recent developments have seen the release of Intel's Pentium III now offering speeds of up to 600 MHz plus the emergence of Advanced Micro Devices (AMD) as a real competitor. AMD's new offering, the K7, now renamed the Athlon, is claimed by AMD to offer overall speed increases over an equivalent Pentium III of almost 40 percent. Both these devices are at present aimed at the power end of the market and come with prices to match. By the time you are reading this it's quite likely that both companies will have chips that run at speeds of up to 750 MHz.

Processors such as the Pentium III are now running at speeds of up to 600mhz and faster.

What does the future hold? Certainly the explosive growth in use of the Internet and electronic commerce looks set to continue as businesses begin to appreciate the worldwide marketing potential it provides. Also as competition between the Internet service providers hots up we are now seeing dramatic drops in the cost of using the Net thus encouraging more and more people to join in.

A few more years should see games technology reach the point where the graphics are literally indistinguishable from the real thing.

Later versions of software have always demanded faster PCs, with more memory and state-of-the-art components.

Voice recognition technology, which has been slow getting off the ground, will benefit from the processing power of the newest PCs and this is an area in which there will be real progress made.

As far as PCs themselves are concerned, the end of next year should see the 1000 MHz barrier broken. What's the limit here and is there any real point to it? It's getting to the stage where completely new application concepts will have to be developed to take advantage of the almost frightening growth in processing power.

Hard drive technology is reaching the stage now where the mechanical devices grinding away in our PCs will soon be replaced with solid state drives that will, no doubt, offer vastly increased storage capacities.

Whatever, we can all look forward to further rapid growth in computer technology and it will be fascinating to watch all the latest developments as they unfold.

Hardware

Ok, you've made the decision and it is a big decision because computing, as you'll find, isn't a cheap hobby. A PC is what you want. You've raided the piggy bank and discovered how much you can afford to spend. So what's next? Off to the local PC World with money in hand?

Well not just yet, you shouldn't. There's a few things you ought to be aware of before taking the plunge.

Firstly, buying a computer is going to cost you a lot more money than you might at first think because unfortunately the expense doesn't end with the initial purchase. It is in fact only just the beginning.

'Why so?' you might ask. Well quite simply, after the novelty factor has worn off, you are going to ask yourself, what can I actually do with this thing?

Whatever you decide upon you'll discover you need software and this will necessitate raiding that piggy bank again. Then Junior will pester you into buying him Formula One Grand Prix Racing and you'll find that it won't run because the computer's graphics card isn't up to it and so you'll need to upgrade it. They'll all want to try out the Internet of course and it won't be long before you find yourself cringing each time the phone bill drops on your doormat. Needless to say, there's more. Get the picture!

Secondly, before you go anywhere near a PC shop ask yourself if you know anything about the following: motherboards, hard drives, monitors, graphics cards, RAM, DVD, printers, central processing units (CPUs) or modems. Do you know what an Intel Pentium III is or an AMD K7 and the pros and cons of each?

If the answer is no then read on and find out. An in-depth knowledge isn't required just as long as you understand what they are and what they do.

Have you considered the potential situation a year or two hence. The more advanced programs and computer games become, the more resources they demand. To be able to run these applications, PCs need to be ever faster and more powerful. Will your machine be able to cope? The answer is, without question, a resounding no. Take this as read.

It's possible of course that your only reason for wanting a PC is so you can watch some of the Internet's more questionable content. If this is the case all you'll need is a very basic system with a modem that will probably never need upgrading.

Assuming however that you're reasonably well adjusted, at some stage in the not so far distant future you will be needing to upgrade – but *will* your system be upgradable? The chances are that it will be, to some extent at least. Will this be sufficient for your requirements and how will you know?

The issue of upgrading is without doubt one of the most important things you need to consider when choosing your PC and it's one all too many people ignore to their later regret. To find out just what you need to know, keep reading.

Do you want the PC for any specific purpose? Think ahead, is there anything you *might* want it for either now or in the future? A hobby perhaps, a typical example of this is photography. Personal computers are excellent tools for storing, cataloging and with the correct software, touching up photographs. A bit of cogitation at this early stage can save you both time and money.

In order to assist you in making an informed choice and in dealing with sometimes less than scrupulous sales-staff, we are now going to concentrate on the aspects and components of computers you need to know about *before* handing over the contents of that piggy bank.

Monitor

The monitor is one of the most important components of your system and is certainly one of the most expensive but surprisingly is one of the least considered when it comes to evaluating and purchasing a system.

Why this should be is anybody's guess but perhaps it has something to do with the current obsession for processing speed and graphics card capabilities that seems to be predominant at the moment. Certainly it is seen as something which contributes little to the overall power and versatility of a PC system and this, to an extent, is true.

However as anyone who has upgraded from a cheap 14 inch monitor to one of the modern FST (flat screen tube) 17 or 19 inch models, will tell you, it can certainly make a considerable, if not essential, difference to the pleasure of computing. You will be able to fit much more on to your screen thus minimising scrolling, the picture will be sharper, clearer and flicker free. The gamer will get much more from his games and for certain types of work such as image manipulation and CAD, a high quality monitor is essential.

What is a monitor then? Basically it is a device which converts electrical impulses from an external source into a picture. How it does this depends on the type of monitor.

CRT (cathode ray tube) monitors are by far the most common, accounting for approximately ninety-nine percent of the monitors in use today. To put it as simply as possible they work by means of electron guns that produce three beams of electrons, one for each of the three primary colours: red, green, and blue. These beams are directed at the inside of the screen where they hit a layer of phosphor – energising it to produce light. The beams scan the full width of the screen in sequential lines constructing an image. To keep the image 'fresh,' i.e. on the screen, it has to be redrawn continuously and this is achieved by the electron beams scanning the screen about 30 times a second. This is called the monitors refresh rate.

When buying a CRT monitor you should be aware of the way in which monitor manufacturers arrive at the advertised screen size. What they do is measure diagonally across the CRT. However once the tube is placed inside its plastic casing the amount of screen you actually see will be somewhat less.

In the last two or three years LCD (liquid crystal display) monitors have begun to challenge the CRT stranglehold on the monitor market. These work by selectively filtering the light generated by a set of low voltage fluorescent tubes. The screen itself is a sandwich consisting of layers of liquid crystal cells. When a voltage is applied to the liquid crystals, they move accordingly thus allowing light to pass through and be seen on the display. The amount of movement, hence light on the screen, is controlled by the strength of the applied voltage.

When buying a monitor always buy the best one you can afford. These items are not cheap and it makes sense to start with one that will meet your foreseeable requirements.

These are the two main types of monitor displays relevant to the home PC market today. There are others such as Plasma Display Panels and Field Emission Displays but these are unsuitable for home PC use for various reasons, one of which is their enormous cost and so will be disregarded here.

So which do you plump for: CRT or LCD? For most people the choice will be determined by the cost, which means they will be buying a CRT display. A decent LCD monitor starts at about £1000 whereas a good CRT model can be had for as little as £300. What do you get for the extra £700? You will get a pin sharp picture, wonderfully vibrant colours, much lower power consumption and consequently heat output, and a physically much smaller display. Due to the technology employed the LCD monitor can be less than an inch deep compared to around 15 inches for A CRT monitor. The advantages of this are obvious.

However does all this justify the hefty price tag? This really is down to the individual but for most of us the answer has to be no. It also must be said that the better CRT displays produce an image quality that is very nearly as good as the LCD's.

Whichever you choose I would advise you get the largest and best monitor that your budget will allow as, given the price of the things, it's really not a good idea to get one home and then discover you could do with a bigger one.

Central Processing Unit

Using the human body as an analogy, the Central Processing Unit (CPU or sometimes just called the Processor) is the computer's brain, which manipulates all the other components – memory chips, hard drives, monitor, etc, to interpret, control and display your data.

The CPU will typically make up to 15 percent of the price of the PC.

In its most basic form the CPU is a silicon chip about two inches square, integrated into which are some 7 million micro transistors which act as tiny switches. All operations of the CPU are carried out by electrical impulses turning on or off different combinations of these switches. In the binary system used by computers, transistors are used to represent *zeros* and *ones.* These zeros and ones are commonly referred to as *bits* and are the fundamental principle of all digital computers.

But how on earth can something as simple and basic as a mere switch, no matter how many, take your data from a keyboard or scanner and convert it into something meaningful onto your monitor? Think of your computer, for a moment, as a large board. On one side are rows and rows of light bulbs. On the other side of the board are corresponding rows of switches, one controlling each bulb. By throwing say three switches vertically in a line you will illuminate three lights producing the letter I. Other groups of bulbs will produce different letters and by linking them together you will be able to spell out a word, *computer*, as a topical example. This however would be a painfully slow and laborious method of spelling out a message. How much easier it would be if there was another series of switches each of which controlled all the other switches needed to light up the individual letters. Even better we could have yet another set of switches each of which illuminated an entire word. Instead of needing to throw some 60 switches to spell out the word *computer*, the same result could be achieved with just one switch.

The CPU works on exactly this same principle, of combinations of switches controlling other combinations of switches, only on a much vaster scale. By itself however, it can do nothing. All those millions of switches need to be told when to switch themselves on and off and in what order and sequence. These instructions come from the program or *software*. A computer program is essentially just a list of thousands, even millions, of coded instructions.

When you run a program on your computer the list of instructions is copied from the drive the program is loaded on, i.e. Hard drive, CD ROM drive or Floppy Disk drive, to the computer's memory, known as Random Access Memory or RAM for short. Memory can be thought of as millions of numbered storage boxes, each one being known as a 'memory address' and each box can hold one instruction. When the program starts the CPU looks at the first storage box, or address, and carries out the instruction contained therein. Once this is done the processor looks at the next memory address and so on.

Although software instructions are generally very simple, the CPU has the power to interpret millions of them every second. This is a fundamental concept of computing illustrated by the light bulb analogy above – computers can only do very simple things but they can do lots of those simple things very very quickly. The faster a computer runs, the more instructions it can carry out in a second. Processor speed is measured in Megahertz (MHz).

Since the CPU can work much faster than the RAM, it often has to wait for instructions, which has the result of slowing down system performance. To counteract this, the CPU uses an additional memory bank known as 'cache memory', which is separate from the computer's main memory (RAM).

Usually there are two memory caches, referred to as 'level one' and 'level two'. Level one cache is a very small amount of memory which is built into the processor itself and which runs at the same speed as the CPU. Level two cache memory is usually larger than level one and slightly slower, acting as a kind of halfway house between the PC's main memory and the level one cache.

Cache memory is sometimes described by computer manufacturers as 'pipeline burst cache' and the more of it your computer has the faster it will run.

Random Access Memory

Random Access Memory (RAM) is basically a series of numbered storage boxes, each one of which is capable of holding one instruction. These boxes are identifiable because they are numbered, thus allowing the CPU to retrieve information held in them in the order needed to carry out the purpose of the software program.

RAM, along with the CPU, is one of the most important components of the computer as it acts as the interface between the software and the CPU.

When the computer is switched on all the key components of the operating system will be loaded to the RAM chips and as soon as a program is run, its instruction codes are also loaded to the RAM. This means the CPU doesn't have to constantly refer back to the drive on which the program is running and enables it to work much faster.

It is important to distinguish RAM from storage mediums such as hard and floppy disks, CD-ROM drives and tape back-up systems. All of these mediums are permanent storage devices whereas data stored in RAM is only held temporarily. It's lost when the computer is switched off. This is why programs are stored on hard drives as are any files or documents you create. They can be reloaded later as and when required.

RAM is as important as the CPU to the overall speed of your computer. The more it has the faster it will run.

RAM is measured in bytes, where each byte equals eight bits (binary digits) of information. One byte represents a single piece of information such as an individual letter or punctuation mark, and entry level PCs are now being shipped with typically 64 MB of RAM which equates to approximately 64 million bytes or individual characters. This is enough storage to hold about 42 full-length novels.

When you come to choosing your system the minimum amount of RAM you should consider is 32 MB. This will suffice for most purposes but if you intend to use memory intensive software such as desktop publishing programs, music authoring tools or the latest 3D games then you must go for 64 MB. Bear in mind that if you have insufficient memory, many programs will run very slowly, if at all. This is because the RAM will be incapable of supplying the CPU with the information it needs at the speed that it needs. Also as the software's instructions will be competing for limited resources in the memory, frequent crashes could result.

Another consideration with RAM, apart from the issue of speed and stability, is that the more of it you have, the more programs you will be able to run at the same time. As an example you might be a budding author and as such you will undoubtedly find it useful to have your word processor open in one window, an encyclopedia in another and maybe even a Thesaurus in yet another. For these reasons RAM is probably as important as the CPU if you want a fast and powerful computer.

Motherboard

The motherboard is the main circuit board inside your PC and is basically the heart of the system. On this board you'll find the CPU, RAM chips, BIOS chip, battery, support circuitry, bus controllers and connectors. Connected to it are all the disk drives, hardware such as modems, graphics cards, TV cards, sound cards and peripherals such as scanners, printers and loudspeakers. Also on the motherboard is what are known as expansion slots and there should be three different types; three ISA slots, four PCI slots and one AGP slot.

The differences and pros and cons of these will be discussed later, for the moment all you need to know is that these slots enable you to add extra circuit boards to your system and because of this they are an important part of a PC. Typically these boards might be graphics or sound cards, modems, TV tuner cards or memory expansion cards. The presence or absence of these slots determines to a great extent the potential to which a PC can be upgraded.

Graphics Card

Another main player in the overall performance of any PC is its graphics or video card and at the moment these devices are all the rage, due to their importance when it comes to playing the latest resource hungry games.

A 3D graphics card is essential in order to take full advantage of the latest games in terms of speed and performance.

The graphics card is the interface between the CPU and the monitor and takes the signals from the CPU, turns them into an image and then sends it to the monitor to be displayed. The amount of times the card's image is copied to the screen is typically 70–80 times a second, expressed as 70Hz to 80Hz. This is known as the refresh rate.

Another factor influenced by the graphics card is the resolution that the monitor is able to display, the most common being 640 x 480, 800 x 600 and 1024 x 768. In general 14 inch monitors will use a resolution of 640 x 480, 15 inch monitors – 800 x 600 and 17 inch monitors –

1024 x 768. The higher the resolution the more detailed the picture will be. It follows from this that when buying or upgrading your system, if you specify a large monitor i.e. 17 inch or higher, you must ensure that your graphics card is capable of providing a suitable resolution.

There are two types of graphics card available, 2-Dimensional (2D) and 3-Dimensional (3D). 2D cards are perfectly adequate for general PC tasks as there is absolutely no 3D content in any word processor or spreadsheet and relatively little in programs such as painting or desktop publishing. Regardless of how complex the images may be, they're all flat and two-dimensional. However for applications such as photography or video editing you will need a reasonably fast 2D card.

The PC games market today is worth billions to the game manufacturers and as 3D cards are essential to play the latest games, this is where most of the graphic card research and investment goes at the moment. Due to the enormous complexity of producing a realistic 3D image, the processing power required is colossal and puts a strain on even the fastest CPU. For this reason 3D graphics cards are provided with their own microprocessors and memory banks to take some of the load off the CPU.

The best cards at the moment are being supplied with up to 32Mb of memory that enables frame rates of up to 60 per second. This means 60 3D images are being delivered to the monitor every second resulting in very smooth game play.

So unless you're absolutely certain that you will never play a 3D game on your PC or use any application such as CAD (computer aided design), image manipulation or video editing, you should insist on one in any new system you are buying. Failure to do so at this stage will probably mean adding one as an upgrade at a later date.

CD-ROM Drive

A CD-ROM drive is a device that reads the information stored on the surface of a plastic compact disk. This data is contained in a single continuous track burned into the surface of the CD during the recording process that spirals out from the centre to the circumference and is divided into sectors. Controlled by a method called *constant linear velocity*, a motor driven device called a detector projects a highly concentrated laser beam onto the surface of the CD where it follows the data track. The track contains tiny bumps, known for some perverse reason as pits, which reflect the laser beam in a different way to the flat areas surrounding the pits. A light sensing diode that generates an electrical signal for each pulse of light that it receives picks up these differences. This generates a stream of ones and zeroes that are passed to the RAM and then to the CPU.

You can buy special CD-R (Compact Disk Recordable) drives and writable CDs to go with them – see page 157.

The technology employed enables a single compact disk to hold 650Mb. This is enough to store the contents of a full size encyclopedia. What's more CDs are incredibly cheap, costing literally pennies each to produce. Because of these two factors they are at present the favoured medium for distributing software and have largely superseded their predecessor, the floppy Disk.

Like with most good things though, there is a drawback. Namely, they can only be read from, not written to. This means you can read data they contain but you cannot add data to them. Hence the name CD-ROM, the ROM standing for read only memory.

DVD Drive

A relatively recent development of the CD-ROM disk is a disk known as a *digital video disk* or DVD for short. This works on the same principle as the ordinary CD but the technology has been enhanced so that the data pits burned into the DVD's surface are much much smaller, enabling many more of them to be created thus increasing the data holding capacity. Also the DVD laser uses light with a much smaller wavelength that makes the laser beam narrow enough to accurately read these smaller pits. Furthermore the DVD contains two data layers thus doubling its already vastly increased storage capacity. As if this wasn't enough, both sides of the disk can be used thus doubling its capacity yet again. This opens up whole new possibilities for software manufacturers and is definitely the storage medium of the future. So vast are the storage capabilities of these disks, typically as much as 18 Gigabytes, that the software doesn't yet exist to fully utilise their potential. About the only application that comes close, are DVD movies, typically full-length feature films.

More and more though, memory intensive applications such as encyclopedias are starting to be shipped on these disks and it's only a matter of time before the software manufacturers find ways to fully exploit their amazing capacity. A further advantage of these new drives is that they are quite capable of reading ordinary CDs. So anyone thinking of buying a new PC, would be well advised to specify a DVD drive on their system as it's only a matter of time before they totally supersede the ordinary CD-ROM Drive.

Floppy Disk Drive

While the storage capacity of a floppy disk is only 1.44 Mb it is still an extremely useful storage medium particularly for transporting data from one PC to another. Floppy Disk drives are always labelled 'A'.

With the remarkable developments in storage systems now such as the new DVD drives and hard drives with capabilities of over 30Gb, the old floppy disk seems extremely outdated. Nevertheless, although it can only hold 1.44Mb of information and is somewhat slow in comparison to the other types of drive, it still has several advantages not the least of which is its sheer convenience and dependability. It's probably still the easiest and quickest way to copy data from one machine to another, and when you consider that one floppy disk can hold the contents of a full-length novel, it really isn't to be sneered at. Floppies are also extremely useful as a back up for data saved to hard drives which have been known to become corrupted, or worse, to fail completely. Add to this their cheapness and robust nature and it's easy to see why they are still to be found on virtually all PCs.

As opposed to the optical technology employed in CD-ROM drives, the Floppy disk drive uses electromagnetic principles to store and retrieve data. The Floppy Disk itself is simply a thin Mylar disk, known as a *cookie,* coated with a magnetic film around a central metal core, the whole being enclosed in a rugged plastic case.

Scattered randomly within this magnetic film are millions of tiny iron particles. When writing to a floppy disk an electromagnetic head controlled by electrical pulses from the CPU, scans the surface of the disk creating concentric bands of magnetised particles, arranging them in specific directions. Each band or track is divided into blocks or sectors known as clusters, which hold the data. The number of tracks and sectors and therefore the number of clusters that the electromagnetic head can create on the disk's surface determine the capacity of the disk. When data is retrieved from the floppy, the opposite happens. Instead of the head being magnetised by electrical pulses from the CPU, it is now magnetised by the magnetic field created on the disk during the recording process. This creates electrical pulses which are sent to the CPU for analysis.

Hard Disk Drive

The main storage device in any computer though is the Hard Disk Drive (HDD) and is the one you will access the most. The HDD employs the same electromagnetic principles used in the Floppy Disk Drive only on a much greater scale.

Instead of just one disk as in the Floppy Drive, the HDD has several disks, 4 or more, that are called platters. They are typically made of metal or glass and are coated with a magnetic material.

The hard disk drive is the main storage area of a computer and is usually labelled 'C'. This is where all the computer's main programs will be stored and run from.

At the bottom of the drive, a circuit board, known as a *logic board*, receives signals from the PC and translates them into voltage fluctuations that command the electromagnetic read/write heads to scan the surface of the platters. As in the Floppy Disk Drive, the heads align the iron particles contained in the magnetic coating when writing to the drive and by detecting the changes when reading. The data is contained in millions of numbered storage areas known as clusters. Drives of this type have what is known as a *virtual file allocation table* or *VFAT* and this table is what allows the drive to relocate the data when it is asked to retrieve it. This process works in conjunction with the computer's operating system which reads the VFAT to determine which cluster on the disk holds the first part of the file when reading or which clusters are available to hold a new file when writing. Since one cluster can only hold a limited amount of data, a single file may require hundreds of clusters to store all its data. Due to a process known as fragmentation (discussed later), these clusters are likely to be randomly scattered across several platters which makes file retrieval a potentially tricky operation. To overcome this, when a file is being stored, the operating system orders it to be stored in the first available cluster or clusters as the case may be. The VFAT keeps a sequential record of the clusters used by a file so that the operating system always knows exactly where the data is located and can instruct the read/write heads accordingly when asked to retrieve the information.

When you delete a file the operating system alters the information in the VFAT to indicate that the clusters that were used by that file are now available for reuse. The file data is still on the disk and will remain there until overwritten by another file, so you can often restore – or *undelete* – a file that has been erased.

Hard disk drives are amazing devices and are built to microscopic tolerances. The platters on which the data is stored spin at speeds of up to 120 revolutions a second and the gap between them and the read/write heads are smaller than the thickness of a human hair. The magnetic coating on them is 3 millionths of an inch thick.

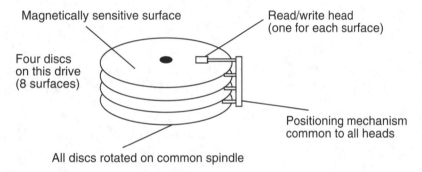

The development of these drives is nothing short of phenomenal. Only 15 years or so ago hard disk drives came with capacities of some 10 megabytes and an access time of about 90 milliseconds. What's more, they weren't cheap. Nowadays HDDs can have capacities of up to 30Gb and can be accessed in less than 6 milliseconds. Not only this but the drives are physically much smaller and their prices are falling in inverse proportion to their ever increasing capacities.

Today PCs are being sold with HDD capacities from 2 to 3Gb at the lower end of the market rising to 15Gb or more at the higher end. A HDD of 6 to 8 Gb is typical of mid range systems and will provide all the storage the average PC user is likely to need. Given their relative cheapness now it would be pointless in settling for anything less.

Keyboard

The Keyboard is another part of the system much taken for granted and most people are quite happy to settle for a cheaper one that most computer manufacturers supply. This needn't be the case however as there are now some quite stylish and ergonomically designed keyboards on the market. On a more practical note, some more upmarket keyboards offer programmable keys and integrated mice and touchpads. If you're willing to spend the money there are even keyboards available that use infrared technology, eliminating the need for a cable.

When you depress a key on your keyboard, you alter the current flowing through a circuit associated specifically with that key. Similarly when that key is released the current changes again. Built into the keyboard is a microprocessor that interprets the changing signals from the keys. Having decided which key has been activated the keyboard processor sends a message to the CPU that will then address itself to the requested task.

The keys on a PC keyboard are largely the same as those found on a typewriter, with a few extra keys.

Enter – is used to confirm your instructions to the PC. Until you depress it the PC will ignore you. You will also use it when writing documents in word processors. In this application it acts like the Carriage Return key found on a typewriter.

Control and Alternative – these two keys can have various functions depending on what application is running. A common use is to perform what is known as a soft re-boot when a PC locks up. This is done by simultaneously pressing these two keys together with the *delete* key.

Function Keys – These are the top row of keys on your keyboard and are marked F1 through to F12. Again, these can be assigned specific tasks depending on what is going on in the computer. PC games make good use of them.

Escape – This is usually used to get out of an application or to go back to a previous screen or option.

Page up, Down, Insert, Delete, and *End* – These keys are usually employed by a wordprocessor and allow the user to scroll up and down a document and to carry out basic editing.

Arrow Keys – These are the four keys marked with arrows, one pointing in each of the cardinal points. One function is to control the movements of the onscreen cursor while another more common purpose is to control the direction of play in PC games.

Print Screen – Pressing this key copies an exact image of your PC screen into the Windows' Clipboard. Pressing it in conjunction with the Alt key captures an image of the currently active window.

Over a period of time keyboards can become dirty inside due to accumulated dust, cigarette ash etc. This results in the keys becoming sticky and difficult to use. With a bit of care the plastic casing of the board can be unscrewed or prised apart and the offending muck cleaned out.

Pointing Devices

A pointing device is essentially a tool that enables you to tell the computer what it is that you want it to do, and the one most certain to be supplied with your PC is the ubiquitous Mouse, so called due to it's vaguely rodent like resemblance. There are other types, principally touch pads where you use your finger as the pointing medium, digitizing tablets which use light pens and trackballs which are basically upside down mice. Game controllers can also be included in this category. Each has its own purpose but for most PC owners the mouse will be the pointing device supplied and used.

Fitted in the base of the mouse is a hard rubber ball that rotates as the mouse is moved, causing two adjacent rollers next to it to turn. One of these rollers is rotated by up and down motion and the other by sideways movement. Attached to each roller is a wheel on which are a series of metal strips that touch a set of contact points as they turn. For each contact between the strips and the contacts, an electrical signal is produced. From this it can be seen that the more the mouse is moved, the greater the number of signals generated. The faster the mouse is moved, the greater the frequency of the signals. These signals are sent to the motherboard where the number, combination and frequency of them are converted into the distance, direction and necessary speed to alter the position of the screen cursor. When the mouse buttons are clicked, more signals are transmitted to the computer and then relayed to the program in use to activate its features.

Scroll More Easily

Raised Back
Fits Your Hand

Zoom Efficiently

The humble mouse has been around for a long time now and its basic design has changed very little. As with the keyboard though, there are more advanced versions available now with features such as scroll wheels, programmable buttons and 'tail-less' models using infrared technology.

For the moment and into the foreseeable future it's difficult to see what can take its place although one possible contender is 'voice recognition' software. This fascinating and potentially wonderfully useful technology, whereby the operator speaks his instructions to the computer is without doubt the shape of things to come and will be covered later on in this book.

Sound Card

Wonderful inventions that they are when it comes to creating and communicating data in the visual medium, computers have yet another ace up their sleeve. We are talking about the medium of sound. PCs are just as brilliant at sound manipulation as they are when dealing with text and graphics. They can't yet cope with the medium of smell, apart perhaps from the unpleasant odour of burnt out chips, but it will probably come eventually.

To do this, just as they need a graphics card to handle pictures, PCs need a sound card. The average user will probably attach a lot less importance to this sound element than he will to the graphics capability of his PC for the simple reason that he's looking at his computer for most of the time, not listening to it. Probably for this reason the sound cards supplied with the average computer are usually on the basic side. This is in stark contrast to the visual medium, where the manufacturers are now supplying PCs with the latest 3D accelerator cards in response to the increasing demand for them, particularly from the gaming fraternity.

However, no matter how basic it might be, any of today's sound cards are more than capable of dealing with the demands made on it by the typical PC application such as playing the little tunes and jingles that Windows likes to put out now and again. Another instance in which lower quality sound cards are perfectly adequate is that of multimedia where many videos are accompanied by a sound track.

Sound cards are usually supplied in the form of an expansion card which be will plugged into the motherboard via a PCI slot. This has the obvious advantage that if you want to upgrade the card; all you have to do is swap the cards over. Some PC systems, very often the cheaper ones, come with the sound card and very often the graphics card as well, as an integral part of the motherboard. The one advantage of this is that it leaves you with a spare PCI slot that would otherwise be occupied. This increases your up-grading options but you will have to disable the original, usually by changing a jumper setting. Instructions for this will be found in your motherboard manual.

Any sound card no matter how good it is, will only ever sound as good as the speakers it is played through.

Many people though are now taking advantage of the wonderful quality and effects available from the more up-market sound cards. Once again we probably have the gamers to thank for creating the demand. With one of these cards it's quite feasible to transform a PC into a full blown recording studio allowing the user to compose complex pieces of music fully capable of being mixed, edited and re-recorded. It's now possible to duplicate literally any instrument under the sun simply by pressing a few keyboard keys and clicking your mouse.

The basis of operation for any sound card is that of analog to digital conversion. The sound enters the card in analog form, i.e. a sine wave, the frequency of which is fluctuating constantly. A processor called an analog to digital converter (ADC) converts this sine wave into an equivalent digital format consisting of the zeroes and ones with which the PC is familiar. It then passes through a microprocessor that takes the strain of the required processing away from the CPU and also compresses the digital data.

What happens from this point depends on what you are doing. If you are making a recording of the sound, the CPU sends it to the specified drive for storage. If playback is required then the whole procedure is reversed, the digital signals are decompressed, converted back to analog form and sent to the speakers where they are amplified to a level high enough to drive the speakers. This procedure is known as *wavetable synthesis* and is the one used in better quality cards.

Another process used is known as *FM Synthesis*. This involves the use of a special chip on the card in which is permanently stored the characteristics of different musical instruments. When playing a piece of music the card produces a synthesised version that includes the characteristics of the chosen instrument. The output quality of these cards is often low as the stored instrument characteristics are usually somewhat rudimentary.

Musical Instrument Digital Interface (MIDI) is a slightly different technology that was developed with a view to decreasing the size of sound files, which can be enormous. This basically works by only saving instructions on how to play music on electronic instruments, not the actual music itself. One of MIDI's most useful applications is in the way an operator can use his PC to control the output of musical instruments or even a group of instruments. This is known as *sequencing*.

Aside from MIDI performance, the quality of any sound card is largely determined by the frequency at which it samples sounds and by the richness of information incorporated in each split second sample. For example let's assume that we want to record a one-second sample of speech to be played by Windows in response to an entered command. In order to digitise the analog voice, the sound card will split that one-second of speech into a number of minute slices, typically 16,000 that would give a 16Khz sample. For each of these slices in time, the volume, pitch and quality of the sound would be recorded. If, however, only 8000 samples were made, the amount of captured data would be half as detailed – minute pieces of information would be left out. Conversely, if a 32Khz sample were made, the quality would be that much better.

These are the values you will often see sound cards advertised at: 8-bit, 16-bit and 32-bit. A 32-bit card will be able to differentiate twice as finely between levels of pitch, volume and tone quality as a 16-bit card, but the resulting file will be twice as large.

As a final note do remember the old adage that any chain is only as strong as its weakest link. This principle applies equally to sound cards. You can go out and buy the most expensive card in the world but it will only ever sound as good as the speakers through which it is played.

Plug and Play

Plug and play is a relatively new concept that was introduced to try and eliminate the almost nightmarish procedure needed to install and configure a new piece of hardware so that it was compatible with existing system devices.

The problems were caused by the fact that each device needs a line of communication, or channel, to the CPU, and prior to Plug and Play there simply weren't enough of them. The term usually used to describe these channels is *System Resources* and you can get into these via the *Control Panel* and *Display*. Common types of resource are *interrupts (IRQs)* and *direct memory access (DMA)*.

As you would expect from the name, an interrupt butts into whatever the CPU is doing and demands its attention. Now, if due to a lack of available channels, two separate devices are forced to use the same resource, the processor will get confused. When this happens the result is what is known as a *conflict.*

Before Plug and Play came along, installing new hardware to a PC could be a somewhat tortuous process, involving endless fiddling about with settings and constant re-booting to see if all the tweaking had had the desired effect which often it hadn't.

To overcome this all the major PC manufacturers, together with Microsoft and Intel, pooled their resources to try and come up with a better system and the end result was called Plug and Play. The theory behind this new concept was to set a uniform standard which all PC component manufacturers would stick to with the intended result that the computer's BIOS (see page 49), Windows operating system and the hardware itself would integrate nicely and thus eliminate these irritating conflicts.

Your PC's Bus

Your PC, when in use, may seem calm from the outside, but it's actually a hive of activity inside. Millions of minute pieces of data are constantly dashing to and fro, all looking for a home. It's like your worst traffic nightmare, but a thousand times worse. All those millions of bits will be whizzing about on the PC's road system (just like us they need a structured means of travel). If you open up your PC and study the motherboard you will see that it contains a maze of tiny silvery tracks. These tracks or circuits comprise the card's road system. The tracks converge at the motherboard's sockets. Plugged into these sockets are other circuit boards known as expansion cards. Typically these will be graphics card, modem, and sound card. All these cards have their own system of roads and so we end up with an extended network of roads. If you look at the system's drives you'll see that they also are connected to the motherboard by means of ribbon cables thus extending the network even more. The same applies to any external hardware you have, these will be connected to the expansion cards at the rear of the system case. All these countless thousands of silver tracks, or traces, as they're known, integrate into a highly organised communications network of almost unbelievable sophistication. In computer terminology this network is called the PC's bus.

This concept of a road network which can be easily extended was first dreamt up in the early 1980's, and proved to be so efficient and adaptable that for a long time it saw little change. Recent developments though have seen the introduction of several different bus types.

The first major change was to increase byte transfer capabilities from 8 to 16 and to accomodate this expansion cards were supplied with more connectors. The new bus, ISA (Industry Standard Architecture) is still to be found in today's PCs albeit combined with other types. The main problem with this system is that it is slow, only able to transfer data at 8Mb a second.

The most commonly used bus at the moment is the PCI (Peripheral Component Interconnect) bus. This system can handle transfer rates of up to 132 Mb per second and is also compatible with Plug and Play.

It is a fact though that even the PCI standard is struggling with today's fast processors. This is more of a problem for the games industry than the average PC user for whom PCI provides acceptable data transfer speeds. In response to the gamers' needs, the industry came out with AGP (Advanced Graphics Port) in 1997. This is a bus system designed to be used by 3D acceleration cards. It comes in the form of a special socket on the Motherboard into which the accelerator card is plugged.

Computer Ports

You can buy all the hardware devices you like, printers, scanners, remote, drives, modems, etc., but in order to make them work you must have some way of connecting them to your PC. This is where your computer's ports, that baffling array of different shaped sockets found at the back of your PC, come into play.

These come in various types, such as the Parallel Port, the Serial Port and the Universal Serial Bus (USB). Let's take the first two. The parallel port is most commonly associated with printers; indeed it is very often referred to as the printer port. Its big advantage is its data transfer speed, some 8 times faster than the serial port.

This port uses cables containing eight parallel wires, hence its name. A serial port in comparison uses only one wire for sending data and one for receiving it. The advantage of the serial port is its simplicity and because of this it can be used with literally any type of hardware device. A typical use for this port is to connect up the mouse that doesn't handle significant amounts of data.

The manufacturers don't supply too many ports, typically two of each, because of the limited amount of space available at the rear of a PC. In your enthusiasm it's all too easy to end up with more hardware than you can physically connect to your PC.

 USB sockets allow up to 127 devices to be run from one socket by linking them together in a process known as daisy chaining.

A recent boon with regard to this problem has been the introduction of the Universal Serial Bus. This system enables you to run no-end of devices (127 actually), from one port by linking them together in a process known as *Daisy-chaining*. Another big plus for USB is the ability to hot-swap. This means you can plug and unplug to your heart's content while the PC is running. With parallel and serial ports you must switch off the PC before you add or remove any hardware. If you don't you'll pay a price.

There are also other types of port, such as the system's drives. Most commonly used types in this application are the EIDE (Enhanced Integrated Drive Electronics) and SCSI

(Small Computer System Interface). The most popular one here is the EIDE mainly because of its comparatively low cost. SCSI shifts data considerably more quickly but is consequently more expensive. If you browse through the big adverts from the hardware suppliers who advertise in the computer magazines you will notice that SCSI hard drives are twice or three times the price of comparatively sized EIDE drives.

Another big advantage of SCSI is that it also has the same daisy-chain method used by USB. SCSI technology isn't just limited to hard drives however. Readily available are what are known as SCSI adapters. These come in the form of an expansion card and plug into one of your PC's expansion slots and as already mentioned above, allow you to connect up to seven separate devices to your PC. Obviously the devices themselves must conform to the SCSI standard. These adapters are not cheap but if speed is of the essence to you, they will significantly boost the performance of your hardware.

Buying Your PC

By now you will have a basic knowledge of a PC's components and what they do. You've considered what you want your system for and thus you know what you *want* in your system. For the sake of the argument let's say you're a self-employed kitchen designer, so you'll use your PC to write letters, invoices and keep your accounts. For this you'll need a decent Office suite such as Lotus Smartsuite or Microsoft Office. A printer will be required to convert it all to paper. You'll also need a large hard drive to store all those graphic intensive kitchen designs. You're also a big kid at heart so when you've done your accounts you'll get your flight simulator out. This means you're going to need a fast PC with plenty of memory and a good 3D graphics card.

It really is important that you know all these things, as you'll soon discover when you enter the computer shop. Most buyers who don't will end up with a system that most closely matches what they *think* they need, usually meaning that they end up paying for things they *don't* need and without things they *do* need. Fortunately this won't be the case with you.

Now you are ready. The next question is where do you buy your PC? Here you have several choices. The nearest and most convenient will be the high street chains such as Dixons. Go a bit further and you'll find the out of town superstores. There's not much to pick and choose between these two although you'll probably have less choice at somewhere like Dixons as they sell other things as well. Computers in these stores will usually be sold as previously configured systems that cannot be altered. This means that if your requirements are specific you are unlikely to find exactly what you want. The reason they do this is that it enables them to shift old stock that they would otherwise be unable to sell. Not only can the unwary end up with a slightly obsolete computer, he will pay more for it here than anywhere else. The sales-staff in these places are sometimes the least knowledgeable about PCs. On the plus side you can try out the equipment before you buy and if you *do* decide to buy, take it home with you immediately.

Probably a better place to go is a local independent computer shop. Here they will build you a system exactly as you want it and probably at a lower price to boot. You'll also be dealing with people who are genuine experts in their field and who will give you excellent advice. You'll almost certainly have to wait two or three weeks though before you receive the system and there'll be no opportunity to try it out beforehand.

Once you have entered the store of your choice this is where things get more interesting. The first thing a good PC salesman will ask you is what you intend to use your computer for. If you can give him a specific answer this will narrow things down immediately. Unfortunately he's not necessarily going to try and sell what's best for you but probably what's best (more profitable or convenient) for him. Make him think right from the start that you are familiar with computers (he won't know *how* familiar). Ask if the systems he is selling come with Intel or AMD processors, are they fitted with USB sockets, how many spare PCI slots do they have? He'll immediately treat you with more respect and be much less likely to try and pull the wool over your eyes.

Most systems will come with various peripherals. Typically these will be in the form of so-called *free* printers, scanners, digital cameras etc. Don't be fooled. These items are most certainly *not* free and will be built in to the price of the system. Ask yourself if you will actually use any of them, a digital camera for example. If the answer is no you are spending money to no good purpose. Also be aware that these items are often of low quality, and worse, very often are last year's model. Don't be shy of asking just how current they actually are.

Another scam is to offer a stack of 'bundled software' at extra cost. Typically this will include 3 or 4 games and a whole host of multimedia titles such as: will making, cookery, languages, encyclopedias etc. The catch with these is that, as with the free printer and scanner, they are usually well out of date, of low quality and of questionable use to you.

One of the most important things you must establish before parting with any money is to determine to what extent your chosen system will be upgradable.

When buying a PC ensure it has the capacity to be upgraded. This can save a lot of time and money at a later date.

You need to ask four questions here:

1 – Will the Motherboard accept the next generation of CPUs?

2 – How many spare PCI slots are there?

3 – Does it have an AGP slot?

4 – Does it have any USB sockets?

If the answer to the first is no then when you eventually decide that you need a faster PC, instead of just replacing the CPU, you will also have to replace the motherboard itself. This is a tricky and consequently expensive operation. The more spare PCI slots, the better. You should have around four. These slots enable you to add extra hardware to your PC. Typically these would include such things as sound and video cards, modems, TV tuner cards, etc.

AGP slots are specifically designed for graphics cards and enable them to work much better and your motherboard should have one of these. Unless you are a dedicated gamer however and want the best possible performance from your graphics card, one of these isn't essential as all graphic card manufacturers provide versions that will plug into a PCI slot. USB (Universal Serial Bus) is the latest system for connecting peripherals to your PC and without doubt the best both in terms of data transfer speed and practicality. Your PC should have at least one.

When choosing your system ask plenty of questions and don't allow yourself to be fobbed off with vague answers.

Everything the salesman promises becomes a term of the contract. Also if you can specify a particular purpose for your PC, it becomes an implied term of the contract that the product will be suitable. If after getting it home, this turns out not to be the case, you have every right to return it and get a refund.

Having decided what you want, now comes the next scam. The salesman will try and sell you an extended warranty. They will usually put as much, if not more, effort into selling you this as the PC itself. Don't fall for it. These policies are vastly overpriced for what they offer. Your local insurance broker will provide the same cover for a fraction of the price. When it comes to paying, if at all possible use a credit card. If your supplier fails to deliver for any reason, you can get a full refund from the credit card Company. Finally remember that with PCs, as all other things, you get what you pay for. At the time of writing there are systems available for as little as £500 and while some of these can be good deals, to achieve these prices manufacturers are doing more than just cutting corners. Components will be low quality and outdated, peripherals and software will be cut to the minimum and service backup probably non-existent. If all you want are word processing facilities and the ability to play basic games, these will be adequate. But if the computer bug bites you, you will find these systems often cannot be upgraded without major expense so they are very restricting.

Another way to purchase your PC is through the mail-order suppliers who advertise in Computer magazines. Buying in this manner makes it easier to shop around and will usually get you more for your money. On the other hand you don't even get to see what you're buying before forking over the readies and you also run the risk of getting involved with some unscrupulous people.

The other type of mail order company is the product vendor who sells directly to the end customer by mail. With some vendors, such as Dell, you can buy their products directly. These manufacturers claim that by selling direct rather

Most direct vendors, like Gateway 2000 don't manufacture PCs from scratch. They shop around for the best value components and simply put them together under their own badge.

than through computer dealers they can offer lower prices. They can save the middleman's profits, and pass them on to you. They also claim that, this way they can have a direct relationship with their customers and provide better technical support. This is quite true with some of these companies. Dell's technical support, for instance, is rated quite highly in the industry. However, not all computer vendors selling direct can be rated so favourably.

Some mail order companies do not advertise but send details of their products or services directly to you by post. They usually obtain your details by renting a customer list from magazine publishers or other companies from whom you may have purchased something.

If you choose to buy your computer, software or other accessories by mail or telephone, it is wiser to use a credit card rather than sending a cheque. Should you have a dispute with the supplier, or should the company suddenly disappear and you have not received your goods, it may then be possible for you to get the credit card company to help you resolve the matter or provide you with a refund.

When you have bought your new computer system check that all the parts are delivered and intact. Check that everything is working. If you have any problems, contact your supplier immediately.

Complete and send all the registration cards to the appropriate vendors straightaway. If you fail to register, you may have problems getting support. Also, with software, you will not qualify for upgrades at special prices, often offered to existing registered customers.

If you are the type that likes to shop from the comfort of a chair, then why not use the Internet! Obviously, you will need a computer connected to the Internet – if you have not yet bought your system, then you can try using someone else's or visit a *cybercafé* in your area and enjoy a cup of coffee at the same time.

Use search engines like http://www.yahoo.co.uk to find PC manufacturers, software vendors, etc. and browse through the latest products on their web sites. You'll be able to download some software directly via the Net too.

Windows

This chapter introduces Windows, the operating system that is used on virtually all PCs. All its main features and functions are explained together with some of its more specialised tools and utilities.

Covers

Chapter Two

Introduction

By now you should have a good understanding of the various parts in your PC and what their purpose is. By themselves however they are useless, just as the human body is without its nervous system. The computer needs something to tie them all together, tell them what to do, when to do it and in what order to do it.

Thus we have the computer operating system, software that takes all the individual components and organises and controls them so that they integrate with each other.

Windows 98 screens are shown in this book. If you have a different version of Windows there may be some differences.

In this chapter we shall concentrate on the Windows operating system, as this is the one most likely to be on your PC.

Regardless of the type of operating system on your computer, before the PC can be used it needs to be *booted*, i.e., brought to life. During this procedure the operating system and various hardware components are 'discovering' each other and establishing a good working relationship that will enable them all to co-exist happily together.

See the appropriate Windows book in this series for further help using Windows.

Once up and running you will then be presented with the Windows interface. Although Windows is essentially very simple, which is just one reason for its continued popularity, initially it does take some getting to grips with. Not only can it do many things but it also provides various ways to do them. An in-depth treatment of this subject would fill the pages of an entire book, so by necessity we are restricted here to a more concise description of Windows, its basic principles of operation and applications.

Booting Up

Before getting into the mechanics of Windows let's first analyze what happens when you switch on your PC.

On hitting the power switch what was an inert and totally useless amalgamation of metal and plastic, slowly comes to life. It's still pretty groggy, much like someone coming to the morning after a heavy night on the town and trying to get themselves back in some semblance of working order.

During this waking up process or *booting* as it's known, the PC is examining itself to see what hardware it has and testing them to see that they are working correctly. It's also checking that the CPU and the RAM are functioning as they should. This part of the procedure is called the *power-on-self-test*, or POST, for short and upon successful completion, a short beep will be heard.

The boot program is contained within a ROM chip on the Motherboard called the *BIOS (Basic input/output System)* and following the POST it executes initialisation routines that identify and configure the different parts of the system. This completed BIOS now looks for the whereabouts of the system files, looking first in the floppy drive and then the hard disk. When it finds them it copies them to RAM from where the CPU can access them quickly. These files contain everything necessary to set up the system, and its default parameters.

Next, the boot program configures and installs all the PC's hardware and their control programs, or *device drivers* as they are called. If these drivers are missing the associated hardware will not function correctly, if at all.

By this stage, assuming all has gone well, your PC will have shaken off its inertia and will be fully alert and ready to do something useful. The monitor will now be displaying the Windows desktop.

The Windows Desktop

The **desktop** is the first thing you see when Windows is loaded and on it you will see various *icons,* each one representing a program or folder. Most of the screen will be blank which allows you plenty of space to customise the desktop with program icons of your own choice.

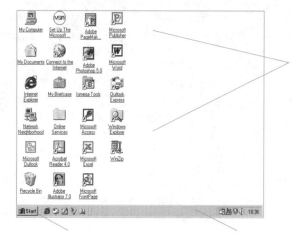

Icons: Windows places some by default as shortcuts to specific programs. You can also add new ones for the programs you want.

Start Button: gives you entry to your PC.

Taskbar: consider this as the control centre. It can be moved to any edge of the desktop horizonally or vertically.

Left click on the icon called *My Computer* and you will see a new screen, again with various icons.

Left clicking on the icons marked A, C and F will reveal the contents of the floppy, hard and CD-ROM drives respectively.

The printer icon will show details of any printers connected to your system and will allow you to configure them.

Control panel reveals another set of icons that can be used to modify the settings of components in your PC and access information about your system.

 Should you delete a file by mistake, the recycle bin gives you a second chance by allowing you to retrieve it. Simply right click on a file and left click *restore.*

Recycle Bin is a useful feature that allows you to delete programs and files from the system without eradicating them permanently. This means that until you empty the bin itself any deleted files will still be on the drive. The whole point of this is to provide you with a safety net, which gives you a chance to retrieve your file if you change your mind or discover you've deleted the wrong file. This is something we all do on occasion so it's a feature worth having. To permanently delete a file, left click the Recycle Bin, select the file to be deleted, click **file** and then **delete**. Even then you will be asked for confirmation so you really have little excuse for making mistakes here.

Right clicking on the desktop icons produces drop-down menus offering various useful options such as **Delete**, which sends the icon's application to the recycle bin, **Open** or **Explore** which reveals the contents of the application and **Properties** which typically tells you the size of the application in Kilobytes, how many files it contains, when it was created, last accessed, etc.

The Start Button

Any of the applications on your PC can be started by clicking on the Start button.

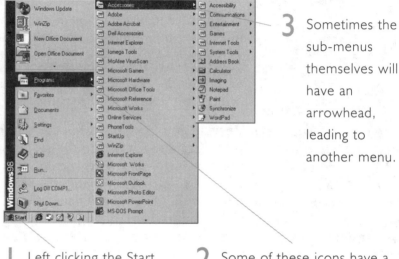

3 Sometimes the sub-menus themselves will have an arrowhead, leading to another menu.

1 Left clicking the Start button reveals the Start Menu, displaying another set of icons.

2 Some of these icons have a little arrowhead to their right that tells you that a sub-menu exists.

Shut Down is your way out of the PC and left clicking here will give you various options. Shut Down itself is fairly self explanatory, **Restart** allows you to reload Windows without actually switching the PC off. **Restart in DOS-Mode** allows you to access the DOS operating system and depending on the age of your PC, you might have a **Suspend** or **Hibernate** option as well. These latter two are part of power management systems found on the latest computers and allow you to put your PC to 'sleep' in the same way as your television can be put on Standby. In this state your PC is on but its main elements, namely the monitor and hard drive, are powered down. This feature allows you to leave programs running and a click or slight movement of the mouse will restore the PC almost instantaneously.

Run provides another way to open applications by typing the full drivepath in the box provided. You'll soon notice that Windows allows you to carry out many of its more basic commands such as opening, closing, and deleting, in a variety of ways.

Help gives you access to Windows' comprehensive help section and here you will find answers to many of your questions although it must be said that much of the information it contains is somewhat on the brief side. The troubleshooters you'll find here can be very handy though.

Find assists you in finding the location of files or programs regardless of where they might be on your system and is another extremely useful Windows tool.

Settings provides another route to the Control Panel and Printers. Also on this menu you will find **Taskbar & Start Menu** that enables you to customise your Taskbar and Start menu by adding or deleting items, although there is an easier way, which we'll see later. **Folder Options** is a tool with which you can customise your folders and their associated icons. **Active Desktop** is another useful application, which you can use to control the way Windows appears on your screen. You can customise the desktop's background, i.e. instead of the rather dull green that Windows uses as its default, you can have any colour you like. Alternatively you can use one of the Wallpapers supplied by Windows, or if you prefer, use one of your own.

A point worth making here is that although PCs are really intended to be workhorses, they can also be great fun. Due to the streak of individuality that makes us what we are, we all like to have things set up in our own way. Just take a look at the horrible zig zaggy wallpaper that your son insisted on for his bedroom, by so doing he's stamped his personality on the room and as adults we are no different. Windows is an extremely user friendly operating system that allows us to fiddle and tweak away to our hearts content. This topic is covered more fully later.

Favorites (American spelling) is a folder in which you can place your favourite files and Internet addresses so you can access them more quickly and easily.

Documents shows a list of files recently accessed and provides a quick way to re-open them again.

Programs shows a list of applications installed on your computer and provides a quick way of accessing them. Essentially it's a shortcut, the program files themselves are elsewhere in your system. If you try deleting from here all you are doing is removing the shortcut, the program files themselves will be left intact. Clicking on a programs icon will open it in a new window.

Wordpad is a straight forward but effective word processor that is perfectly adequate for producing simple documents.

Windows comes with various applications and tools that can be accessed from Programs and these can be found under **Accessories**. These include such things as a handy calculator, some games and a simple but surprisingly useful word processor called **Wordpad**.

Paint is a basic graphics program, which allows you to play around with pictures and create drawings, but as you will see in the section on software there are many far superior graphics applications available. **System Tools** provides an array of maintenance and information tools many of which are useful, some not so. These will be covered in more detail later on.

Windows Explorer and My Co

...cont'd

Windows Explorer, as its name suggests, pr
with a way to fully explore the contents of l
While the Start menu gives you access to s
it is not intended to show you everything i
already mentioned it is merely a system of shortcuts to y
more commonly used applications. When you consider that
there are literally thousands upon thousands of files and
folders lurking about in the innards of your PC, and not all
stored on the same medium either, you begin to appreciate
the need for something like Windows Explorer.

Opening Explorer takes you into a completely different view
of your system's files and folders, showing you the entire
contents of your PC in an easy to follow hierarchical
structure. This enables you to find anything on the system,
and more conveniently, all from one window.

All your PC's
drives are
listed here
along with
some of the
system's
more
imortant
applications.

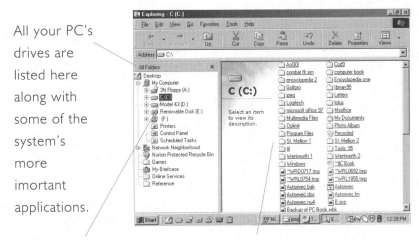

Left click on a drive and
the folders it contains are
displayed on the right.

Left clicking on the folders
will reveal their contents in
the form of files.

1 To start Windows Explorer, right-click on the Start button, then select *Explore* from the pop-up menu.

2 You should see a window split into two panes. The pane on the left illustrates the hierarchical structure of the system, while the right-hand pane shows the contents of whatever folder or medium is selected on the left.

3 To navigate the contents of your hard drive, use the scroll bar at the right of the left-hand pane to move down the hierarchy until you see a grey box-like icon labelled with the letter that represents the hard disk (normally C:).

4 Click on this, and the contents of the first hierarchical level of the drive will be displayed in the right-hand pane.

The right-hand pane should consist of a number of folders, and perhaps some files. Folders are represented by an icon of a yellow loose-leaf folder, and may contain files or further sub-folders. Files, which may be programs, documents or elements used by those programs, have their own customised icons depending on what they are. To see the contents of a folder, double-click on it in the right-hand pane. To start a program, or to open a document, double-click on the appropriate icon.

Explorer is not just a tool to help you survey the catalogue of your files; you can also use it to move files to different locations, copy them and delete them.

To **move** a file from one location to another, or to **copy** it, click on it with your mouse to select it, then drag it over to the new location.

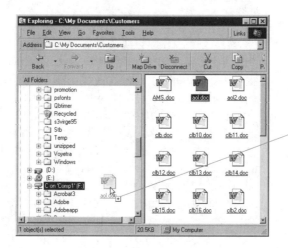

The plus sign next to the cursor here indicates that the selected file is being copied, not moved.

Before releasing the mouse button, check the appearance of the pointer. If it appears as a normal arrow, then you are about to perform a Move operation; if it appears as an arrow with a plus-sign in a box near the arrow's tail, then you are about to Copy. The initial state of the pointer depends on where you want to move/copy the file from and to. If the home and destination of the file are on the same drive, then the default operation will be a Move; if they are on different drives, then the default will be a Copy. Release the mouse button if the action you want to perform is indicated. Otherwise, press Ctrl to copy the file, or Shift to move it – then release the mouse button.

If you want to move or copy a group of files rather than a single one, press Ctrl while clicking on each file successively – then click on any of the highlighted files and drag as normal.

To **delete** a file, a group of files or a folder, select it, then press the Delete key.

Another way of examining the folders and files on your system is to use My Computer – double-click on the icon on the desktop. This fulfils a similar function to Windows Explorer, except that the display uses only one pane, giving perhaps a clearer and simpler view of a folder, but not allowing you to copy and move files so easily.

Maximising, Minimising and Resizing

On the top right hand side of all windows you will see three small boxes. Clicking on the first box marked with a minus sign will minimise the window down to the taskbar but leave the application running. Clicking its button on the taskbar will restore it. The middle box marked with a square enables you to alter the size of the window to either maximum or actual size. In its minimised position the window can be resized to any size you want by moving the cursor to the edges and corners of the window, left clicking with the mouse button held down and dragging the window to the required size. Left clicking and dragging on the blue bar at the top of the window will allow you to position the window where ever you want. Clicking on the box marked with an X closes the program completely.

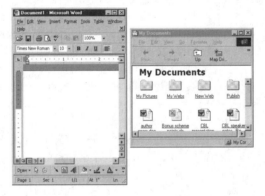

The purpose of this facility to resize and move open windows becomes clear when you have more than one program running at the same time. Each application will have its own window and to be able to see what's going on in each you need to be able to view all the windows simultaneously. To achieve this Windows allows you to position and resize all of them to suit your requirements. A typical example of this would be a writing application that requires research. Your wordprocessor would be open in the main window, in a second smaller window could be the contents of an encyclopedia. Both are available to you at the same time, thus speeding up your work considerably.

Installing Programs

Before any program can be used it first needs to be installed and there are several ways to do this. Windows itself provides a tool called *Add/Remove Programs* that you will find in the *Control Panel*. This is very easy to use; simply follow the instructions Windows gives you.

Another method is to use the application's own *install* feature. Assuming you are installing from a CD, place the CD in the CD-ROM drive and the auto-run feature should reveal the application's interface on the screen. Here you should see an *Install* button. Click it and the program will be installed for you. You will also be allowed to choose which drive you want the application installed to and more specifically, exactly where on the drive. If you see a *customise* feature, this will allow you to select which elements of the program you want installed.

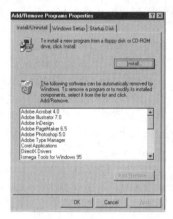

If for any reason *Auto-run* doesn't open the CD's interface, go into *My Computer*, left click the CD-ROM drive and the CD interface will open. Another way is to right click the drive, then left click *Open*, which will display the contents of the CD. A bit of exploration should soon reveal an icon marked *Install* or *Set-up*. Left click and you're away.

Another option is to go into the *Start Menu* and click *Run*. In the box provided, type the name of the program's installation file. However the above methods are easier.

Opening and Closing Programs

Having installed your program you now need to run it. Unless you specified differently during the installation, it will be found under *Programs* on the *Start Menu*. Scroll through the applications listed and when you find the one you want left click to open it. To exit a program simply click on the X box at the top right hand corner. Alternatively, click *File,* then *Exit*.

Files and Folders

Windows allows you to create, delete, customise, move, and store files. If you've lost a file it can help you to re-locate it. It can hide private files or let you password protect the PC itself.

To create a folder, go to the drive where you want the folder to be stored, left click *File*, point to *New* and left click *Folder*. The folder must have a name so you can find it again – so type a name for it in the box underneath. If at any stage you want to give it a new name, simply right click on it and go to *Rename*. You'll also notice that right clicking on a folder shows a range of other options as well, many of which are replicated from the *File* menu. This allows you to manage your folder without actually opening it. When using Windows, your filenames can be up to 255 characters in length. You mustn't however use any of the following symbols: ? " \ / < > : * | as Windows won't accept them.

Having created and stored your folder you might want to place it elsewhere. Windows provides several ways to do this: highlight the folder, go to *Edit* and click *Cut* to move the folder or *Copy* to copy it. Open the destination folder and under *Edit* click *Paste*. The folder will appear in its new location. If you want to move a number of folders, highlight them by holding down the *shift* key while you make your selection. To move all the folders click *Select All* from the *Edit* menu. Or right click on the folder to be moved and *Cut* or *Copy* from the menu that appears.

Drag and Drop

This subject brings us to one of Windows most user-friendly features, namely, *Drag* and *Drop*. The procedure is simplicity itself. To move a file from one folder to another, you need to have both the origin folder and the destination folder in view at the same time. Resize them as necessary, then in the origin folder select the file to be moved, hold the left mouse button down and simply drag the file across to a position within the destination folder. Hey presto, the file is moved. Using the right button in the same way gives you the option of either moving or copying the file. A third option offered here would be to leave the file in its original place but create what's known as a *shortcut* in the destination folder. Clicking on the shortcut will open the file just the same as if it had been moved. These shortcuts are identified by a little black arrow within a white box in the bottom left hand corner of the application's icon.

Windows
Explorer

Drag and Drop does more than allow you to move files and folders however. Using this method you can move nearly any program from anywhere in the system to the desktop or taskbar from where they can be instantly accessed. Typically you would do this with programs you use the most. There are things you can't Drag and Drop however. For example, if you try to move the *Floppy disk*, *Hard disk* or *CD-ROM* drive, *Control Panel*, *Printers* or *Dial-Up Networking* from My Computer, you'll find that you are not allowed to do so. You will instead be presented with an option to create a shortcut to these.

Customising Your Desktop

You can rearrange your desktop icons by right clicking the desktop, left clicking *Arrange* Icons and removing the check sign from *Auto Arrange*.

Here Windows presents you with two main options: Web style or Classic style. If you prefer you can combine elements of both by choosing a third option, *Custom*. This menu is available by left clicking *My Computer, View, Folder Options*.

Windows has been designed to integrate seamlessly with the Internet. There are so many different ways you can browse the web – from Windows Explorer, from within any folder, using Internet Explorer, Favorites, etc...

Apart from the options presented above, Windows allows you to customise the desktop with limitless combinations of colour, pictures and patterns, many of which Windows provides itself. Alternatively you can use your own pictures or patterns that can be scanned into the PC (for which you'll need a scanner), or composed with a graphics application such as *Paint*.

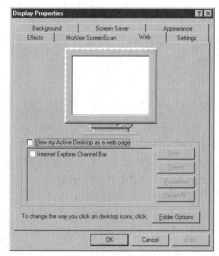

Another way to access your customisation tools is to right click on the desktop, select *Active Desktop* and then *Customize My Desktop*.

To access the customisation tools, click *Start*, go to *Settings, Active Desktop* and then *Customize my Desktop*.

Background displays a list of wallpaper that Windows provides which you can use to decorate your desktop.

Appearance presents you with a range of predetermined colour schemes plus the option to customise your own.

Screen Saver allows you to choose one of Windows' screensavers. The original purpose of screensavers was to protect the monitor screen from having an image 'burnt' into it by a stationary application. These days with the improvement in monitors, this consideration is less of an issue and screensavers are now used more for entertainment than anything else.

Settings allows you to adjust the colour depth of the monitor's resolution and also the size of the display.

These are Windows' basic operating features and learning them will soon have you reasonably comfortable with the system. When you are, you will be ready for the next section.

Windows Applications and Tools

There's more to Windows than simply being an efficient filing cabinet. Just as in any office environment, files and folders get lost, misplaced, or simply dumped in the most convenient place. Periodically the resultant mess needs sorting out and it's no different with Windows, so it thoughtfully provides you with tools for this purpose. You'll also find other tools and programs to check your hardware for problems and keep them running in good order and to get the best out of your system generally. We'll now consider some of these features of Windows which are:

Backup

ScanDisk

Compression Agent

Disk Cleanup

Disk Defragmenter

Backing Up

Get into the habit of backing up your work on a regular basis. This could save you countless hours one day.

Imagine you've just spent all day typing out a document on your word processor. You've set up the document's parameters, fonts, edited it several times and generally taken the time to produce a professional looking piece of work. You are nearly finished and glad of it as your eyes are beginning to turn square. All that remains is to save your work to a drive. Your finger is closing on the mouse button, when the dog, who has been lying quietly on the sofa all day, suddenly decides the cat is invading his space and chases it behind your desk, ripping out your PC's power cable in the process. You give the dog a good kick (metaphorically speaking), plug the PC back in and reopen the word processor. The trouble is that unless you've been periodically backing up your work throughout the day or activated the word processor's autosave function, the document won't be there. You'll have to start it all over again. Irritating or what!

Now this particular scenario might be unlikely (even more so if you don't have a dog), but it serves to illustrate what literally every PC user experiences at one time or another – the sudden and unrecoverable loss of their data. Take it as read that the sudden realisation can come as a considerable shock. It might only be five minutes work or it might be five months work. In a situation like the case above, we might fume for a while but we wouldn't be suicidal about it. But imagine how you would feel if one day your hard drive crashed – permanently. All your data would still be in that little box but there would be absolutely no way for you to get it back out.

The solution is to get into the habit of making regular backups, be it a word document or the data files stored on your hard disk. In the case of a word processor document all you need do is to periodically save to the hard disk. When you've finished for the day make another copy on a floppy disk. Then your work is safe. Alternatively you can use Windows' excellent *Backup* program which you can find under *Start* menu, *Programs, Accessories, System Tools.* This is very easy to use as Windows guides you through the process. All you have to do is select the files you want to backup, where you want to store them; usually a floppy disk or a back up drive such as an Iomega Zip/Jaz. Then click the *Start Backup* button. If the files need more than one disk you will be prompted to insert new ones as required. You can tell how many disks you are likely to need during the file selection procedure, the Status Bar at the bottom of the window will tell you the size of the files in Kilobytes. The importance of doing this on a regular basis cannot be stressed enough as you will realise when you have your first crash.

To restore your files from a backup disk, the procedure is essentially the same only in reverse. The program does the work, all you do is click the appropriate buttons.

 If you haven't already made a recovery disk, stop what you're doing and make one now. It'll only take 5 minutes and requires just one floppy disk. Having made it, do update it periodically.

While on this subject let's take another look at the Recovery Disk that Windows will ask you to make. There is a very good reason it does this. As you move your files around the system, install and uninstall programs, add and remove hardware, etc, your computer will gradually become more and more untidy. Files will be in the wrong place or bits of them will be scattered around or could even be lost completely. If one of these is an important system file you will find that when you switch on your PC one day, Windows will refuse to load. Less seriously you could be having problems with sound, hardware, memory or display. This is when that Recovery Disk, in all probability lurking about at the bottom of a drawer, will be worth its weight in gold.

This disk contains all Windows Start Up files and using it enables you to get the system up and running again. You will be presented with various options and the idea is to try each option in turn to see if the problem has been solved before going on to the next option. There is also an option, which allows you to restore the system completely from a file in Windows called the *Master Image*. This is a compressed copy of every file, including Windows files, that was loaded onto your PC by the manufacturer. This option will first delete *everything* on your hard drive before restoring it again from the Master Image. If you use this option make a separate backup of all your data. As restoring from the Master Image returns your PC to the state in which you received it from the manufacturer, it is an excellent way of clearing all the junk out of your system and returning it to new. Another point to be made when using this option is that it's not just your data that needs backing up but also any *program* that wasn't originally loaded on the PC. Also any device drivers for hardware such as printers and scanners that weren't supplied with the PC will have to be reloaded, so it isn't something you want to do too often. Making the recovery disk is easy and takes around five minutes. All you need is one floppy disk – then just follow the on-screen instructions. It's also worthwhile to update the recovery disk periodically.

ScanDisk

All mainten-ance tools can be found under *Start, Programs, Accessories, System Tools*. Make a point of using them if you want to keep your system running smoothly.

ScanDisk is a Windows utility that is provided for the purpose of checking your drives for problems and errors. It does a physical check of the disk's surface and also an analysis of the way data is stored on it. If it finds problems it can usually repair them. Potential problems are incorrectly addressed data clusters that means the system might not be able to recover the data when asked to do so. Another more serious problem is that of physical damage to the magnetic surface of the disk and when ScanDisk comes across a damaged sector, it simply marks it as 'Bad'. Any files you save subsequently will be kept away from this sector. This is much more likely to occur with removable media such as floppy or Zip disks as these are a lot more exposed to the elements. Fortunately the problem is usually restricted to a few clusters, which relatively speaking is a minute area, and so makes little or no discernible difference to the user. You will find ScanDisk under *Start, Programs, Accessories, System Tools*. Opening the program will present you with the option of two tests – *Standard* and *Thorough*. *Standard* will check all files and folders for errors while *Thorough* will check files and folders plus the surface integrity of the disk. Then you can choose whether to let ScanDisk automatically repair any errors it finds or simply advise you of what it has found.

You will notice that when Windows is shut down incorrectly, the next time it boots, ScanDisk will run automatically, although you can cancel it if you wish. This is Windows playing safe as most drive errors are caused by incorrect shutting down.

As a final note, when running ScanDisk's *Thorough* test, make sure you have something else to do as it can take ages depending on the speed of your PC. Also make sure you have no other applications running, including screensavers, as these can interfere with ScanDisk.

Compression Agent

To understand what this tool does you first need to know just what is meant by the term Compression. Basically there are two types – file compression and disk compression.

Let's take file compression first, a process also sometimes known as *zipping*.

Compressing your files is a good way of conserving drive space. A very popular compression program is one called Winzip, which is available free at: www.winzip.com

The principle behind file compression is that of eliminating *redundancies* in the file being compressed. When the compression program is running it is looking for recurring patterns of data. As an example of this, consider the following masterpiece of prose:

'janet admired the jaunty way that jack was wearing his hat'

Here we have two recurring patterns, firstly, 'ja' written three times and secondly, 'wa' written twice. Having located the patterns, the program deletes them but not before saving an example of each in a special file. It then places a marker to indicate where in the dictionary the pattern can be found. Multiply this process possibly thousands of times in a long file and it becomes clear how the file will be reduced in size.

When your computer comes to read the compressed file, it sees the markers placed during the compression process and *decompresses* that section by retrieving the pattern from the dictionary, thus restoring the file to its original size.

You cannot compress drives further if you've already used Drive Converter to convert to the newer, more efficient file storing system called FAT32.

You can use Compression Agent to compress selected files using the settings you specify. Find it under *Start, Programs, Accessories, System Tools.* You can only use Compression Agent to compress files on drives compressed using DriveSpace 3 – this is the disk compression program which can greatly increase the storage space available for your files, not only on your hard disk but also floppy disks, and it's also available via *System Tools.*

Compressing large number of files or running DriveSpace can be a lengthy process so schedule these procedures for a period when you will not need your computer.

Disk Cleanup

Every time you use your PC things are going on inside that you are simply not aware of. Files are continuously being created, modified and deleted. Windows, for example, creates what's known as a *Temporary File* that it uses as a temporary backup while performing some function or other. This allows you to revert back to the previous set-up if something goes amiss. In most cases Windows erases these *temp files* automatically but sometimes things go wrong – your PC might crash for example, necessitating a re-boot in which case one of these files might remain on the drive.

Browsing through the *Windows* folder will show you the location of the folder which contains these *temp* files, which, not surprisingly, is named *Temp.* Very often specific programs themselves will create temp files and again, as with Windows, are supposed to delete them when finished with. The problem with some of these programs is that many of them are not all that well written and neglect to clean up after themselves. This has the inevitable effect of cluttering up your PC over a period of time with redundant and useless data that eventually slows your system down.

If you suspect someone has been nosing about in your computer, open the *History* sub-folder in the Windows main folder. This will show you what files have been opened and when.

The Internet is an even worse offender in this respect. Within your *Windows* folders you will find one called *Temporary Internet Files*. Take a peek in here after your next session on the Net and you might be amazed at what you find. Everytime you go on the Net, particularly if you are browsing about, all sorts of spurious data will be downloaded to your PC, totally without your knowledge. If you don't clear it out occasionally, this folder will eventually bulge at the seams with rubbish, especially if you are browsing sites with a high graphic content. You might also find stuff in there that would be difficult to explain away and this point isn't made flippantly. It's all too easy to inadvertently stumble across one of the Net's more questionable sites and when you do it will let your PC know you've been there.

The disk cleanup utility provides you with an easy method of ditching all this junk, thus freeing up valuable disk space. You can also empty the recycle bin from here.

Defragmenting

When a hard disk or floppy disk is formatted, it is organised into different areas, each with its own address, which enable the disk controller software to find the position on the disk where it wants to read or record data. When a file is written to disk, the controller software tries to keep all of the file in the same location, so that it will be easy to read back all of the file in one go; but if the file is too large to fit into a single available location, it will be split up and distributed around different areas of the disk, the different sections of data being linked to each other by pointers. This happens increasingly as revised files grow, and as old files are deleted, leaving gaps which must be filled up. The problem with the fragmenting of files is that it results in an extended disk access time, as the drive has to make a new search for each separate part of a file.

Windows comes with a program called Disk Defragmenter, which reorganises the data on your disk so that files are stored in contiguous areas – meaning that only one fresh search is needed for each file that needs to be read or written. To run the program, select Programs>Accessories>System Tools>Disk Defragmenter from the Start Menu. Now select the drive that you wish to defragment, and click *OK*. A dialog box showing the progress is displayed as shown below. If you click on the Show Details button, you are presented with a schematic representation of the different clusters of data on your drive, which you can see being rearranged as Disk Defragmenter does its job.

 A hard drive usually takes around half an hour to defragment, though the time will depend on the speed and size of the drive, and the speed of your computer.

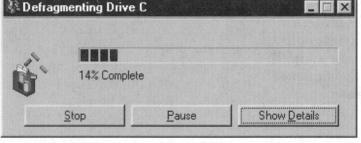

Formatting

Before any disk can be used, it must first be formatted in order to create a file and folder system. Right click on the drive's icon in *My Computer* and then left click *Format*.

Before any magnetic storage medium can be used it must first be formatted. This procedure prepares the disk, i.e. formats it, so that there will be a way for Windows to organise and locate data saved to it. In its unformatted state the disk will have millions of minute iron particles scattered randomly throughout the magnetic film that covers its surface. This however is no good to the PC, it's a logical beast and doesn't appreciate things that aren't. To make the PC like it, the magnetic surface of the disk must be organised into neat sectors and tracks. These act like signposts and tell the read/write heads exactly where to read or write data. Most magnetic media are now supplied pre-formatted but you will occasionally come across some that aren't. If you do you will need the formatting utility available by right clicking on the drive to be formatted then left clicking *Format*. Formatting can also be useful if you want to totally eradicate the data on a particular storage medium, for security purposes maybe. This will completely *blitz* the disk.

Clipboard Viewer

The Paste Special command is used for Object linking and Embedding. Instead of simply pasting the contents of the Clipboard into the active document, Paste Special embeds or links a file made with another Windows application.

This is an invaluable and extremely versatile Windows application that allows you, for example, to move text and graphics from one program to another, take snapshots of your monitor screen and convert file formats.

1 To copy to the Clipboard, select whatever you want to copy, then choose the Copy command from the Edit menu (or right-click with the mouse to bring up a similar, context-specific menu). Selecting Cut instead will move the selected matter to the Clipboard, deleting it from its original location.

2 To paste the contents of the Clipboard later on, simply choose Paste from the Edit menu.

You can also use the clipboard to take photos of your onscreen displays. Simply press the *Print Screen* key that you'll find at the top right of your keyboard, open the clipboard and you'll find a perfect reproduction of whatever happened to be on the screen at the time. If you press the *Alt* key and then the *Print Screen* key, then you'll just capture the active window on the display, the background will be left out. Any snapshots you take can be filed in the usual manner or imported into various applications.

Security

Security is perhaps not much of an issue for the average home PC owner but even so it's a subject worthy of mention.

Firstly, Windows comes with its own in-built security system that prevents you from deleting any of its system files. This is sensible as it's all to easy to delete things by accident, either through tiredness or carelessness.

To lock up your PC entirely, right click on an empty part of the desktop, click *Active Desktop* then *Customize my Desktop, Screen Saver.* Make sure you've selected a screensaver and the time delay you want first. You'll see a box entitled *Password protected.* Tick this and then click *Change.* In the box that appears type in your password and then confirm it below.

As soon as the screensaver runs your PC will be locked. To unlock it just move the mouse slightly and the password box will appear. Enter the password and you're back in.

However, you might find this a somewhat drastic way to hide the contents of what will probably be no more than one file, particularly in a family environment where other people will no doubt want to access the PC. One possibility is to use the password facilities of your word processor, as you should be able to open up a word document, put your secret file in it and then set your password. This won't be so practical though if your file contains graphics.

There is a way to hide files and folders within the Windows system although they won't be password protected and so the level of security will be low. Assuming though that you're not hiding state secrets it should be adequate. The way to do it is as follows: open any Window, left click *View* and then *Folder Options*. You will see another tab called *View*. Left click this and in the list that appears go to *Hidden Files*. Click *Do not show hidden files* and then close the Window. Now right click on the folder you want to conceal, left click *Properties* and then tick the *Hidden* box. Close the window. The next time you open the drive that contains your secret file it won't be on view. You'll know it's there but nobody else will. To access it again reverse the above procedure.

Another simple way is to give your file an obscure name and squirrel it away deep within another folder that contains masses of other folders and files. Just don't forget what you named it though or you might have quite a job on your hands to find it again.

However if you have something that you definitely, absolutely, don't anybody to see, there are commercial encryption programs available which will lock your secrets securely away whilst still leaving your PC available for use.

Deleting Files

This topic merits a little section all of its own because many people don't know how to delete things correctly and this can cause all sorts of problems. The Golden Rule here is if in any doubt at all, do **not** delete. If you do, use your PC for a while to see if anything is not working as it should. If you find something isn't and the problem can be traced back to the deleted file, then restore it from the Recycle Bin. Only when you are certain that all is well, should you empty the Bin.

This subject also requires a brief mention of the Registry. This is a hierarchical database within Windows that the average user will never see and is used to store information concerning virtually everything in your computer. Everytime you add or remove a piece of hardware from your system for example, you are altering the contents of the registry. This also applies to every program that you install on your computer. Now when you come to remove a program, if done correctly, the registry will be amended accordingly and all will be well.

The trouble is that all too many people don't do it as they should. A common mistake is to *right* click on the programs icon in Programs and *delete* from there. All they've achieved by doing this is to remove the program's shortcut from the *Program* menu. The program files themselves will still be on the hard disk. When they realise their mistake and eventually locate the program itself, they do the same again. *Right* click and then *delete*. This time they'll achieve their aim. The program will be deleted. What *won't* be deleted however are the references to the program in the registry. The result of this is that over a period of time the registry becomes clogged up with redundant entries and like any device that gets clogged up, it loses efficiency.

A more serious problem can occur with certain programs, usually cheap ones. These applications *borrow* files from other programs similar in nature, which is all very well until you come to delete them and then find you've deleted the borrowed files as well. This can cause all sorts of headaches so beware.

Better quality software will be provided with their own uninstall program and where supplied should always be used.

In order to do the job properly Windows supplies you with a utility called *Add/Remove Programs* and you will find it in the *Control Panel*. Clicking on this will show you a list of programs installed on your PC. The idea is that from the list, you select the program you want to delete and then click the Uninstall button, if your program is listed, all well and good. The problem with this particular utility is that it's not one of Windows' best features and all too often you'll find that the application you want to get rid of is not in the list. Even if it is listed you'll often get a message saying that Windows was unable to remove the application completely.

Many applications now come with their own Uninstall programs.

So what do you do? You'll need to buy an *Uninstall* program. These work by monitoring the installation of a program, noting any changes made to the system and then when it comes to deleting, they are able to undo those changes leaving the computer exactly as it was originally. These programs are also very useful when it comes to clearing out your system and will often tell you what files are safe to delete and which aren't. Invest in one of these as they are well worth it.

Icons and File Extensions

Icons as you will have already noticed are little pictures or graphics used by Windows to represent different types of file and folder. Programs you install will also be supplied with their own icons and any work you create with these programs will be given the same program icon. Initially you might find the vast range of the icons used by Windows confusing, but as you become more familiar with your PC you will soon be able to recognise the more commonly used ones. As you do you will begin to appreciate just what an efficient way they are of instantly telling you the nature of a particular folder. A list of the icons Windows uses together with the applications they represent can be found in any Window by left clicking *View, Folder Options* and then *File Types*. It's well worth studying these and you will also find the icons for many of the programs installed on your machine in the same list.

Another recognition method used by Windows is that of *file extensions*. You won't find these on folders, just on the files within the folders. These extensions always use three letters, i.e. .doc.

File extensions are essential to the operating system but are of less importance to the user and by default Windows hides them from view. If you wish to see them however, go to *Windows* Exp*lorer, View, Folder Options, View* and then unclick the box marked *Hide file extensions for known file types.*

There are many different types of file and consequently file extensions, some more important than others. One of the ones you'll come across most often is .exe: and this denotes an executable file, which basically is the file needed to open an application. Another common type is .bak: which is used by many programs to create a backup of the previously saved version of the file in use. When a file is saved for the first time it adopts the applications default icon. If you then save the file again, the first file is renamed with the extension .bak: and the new version takes the default extension.

Fonts

A font is a set of all the typeface characters available in a certain style (*italic*) and weight (**bold**), for a particular design. A popular font is *Times New Roman.* Fonts are used by PCs for on-screen displays and by printers for producing hard copy.

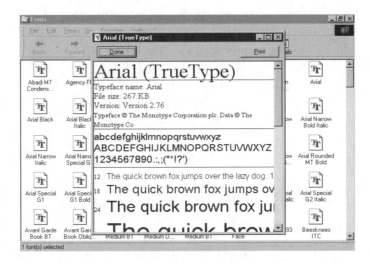

The PC stores these fonts as *bitmaps*, which is basically a series of dots, and the folder in which they are located can be found in the *Control Panel*. Opening the folder will display all the fonts installed on your computer. Clicking on an individual font icon will open a large box in which you can actually see how the font looks. Windows supplies well over one hundred fonts, which will probably be an overkill for the average user, but if you're still not happy, there are a million and one other fonts available out there for you to install. You can also get programs known as font editors that allow you to create your own fonts or to modify existing ones.

Printing

A good deal of the tasks for which you use your computer will be meaningless unless you can print a "hard copy" of your work out onto paper. Printing in Windows is very easy: all applications that allow you to produce printable material will offer a Print command, normally under the File menu. You are then usually presented with a dialog box which allows you to select which pages of a document to print, how many pages, etc. Windows then does all the rest for you – you don't have to configure each individual application to use your printer, since all applications use the same settings you initially provide Windows. To add a printer, or to modify the settings that apply to a printer already installed, select Start>Settings> Printers, then double-click on the appropriate icon in the Printers window.

Another benefit of using a common printer driver for all Windows applications is that you can use any of the fonts installed on your system in any of your applications. To see a list of all the fonts currently available to you, choose Start>Settings>Control Panel, then double-click on the Fonts shortcut icon – or open the c:\windows\fonts folder.

One very easy way of printing a file is to drag the file's icon onto your printer's icon. This can be found in the window summoned by selecting Start>Settings>Printers; alternatively, you may wish to set up a shortcut icon for the printer, on your desktop. To do this, click on the icon in the Printers window and drag it out onto the desktop using the right mouse button, then select *Create Shortcut(s) Here* from the context menu that pops up. Now, all you have to do to print a single copy of the full document is drag its icon out of Windows Explorer, or a My Computer window, and onto this desktop shortcut icon.

The Internet

With the possible exception of computer games, the Internet and e-mail are probably the main reasons why people today are buying personal computers. This chapter explains what the Internet is, how it works and shows you how to get the best out of it.

Covers

Chapter Three

Introduction

It's becoming literally impossible these days to pick up a newspaper or switch on your TV, without having someone exhort you to get a life and get on to the Internet. The terminology bandied about may include such fanciful titles as the World Wide Web, Information Superhighway, Cyberspace or Global Village, but they all come back to the same thing – The Internet.

This modern day phenomenon has its roots in the simple networks to be found in any office, whereby a handful of computers are linked to each other, enabling instant inter-departmental communication, such as e-mail. The Internet is essentially an extension of these basic networks but on a truly global scale.

 See Internet UK in easy steps for a comprehensive guide to using the Net.

The medium most commonly used to connect all the millions of computers that comprise the Internet, is the old fashioned telephone line. This system has its faults but for the moment at least, the telegraphic system is for most people the only realistic way of connecting to the Net.

Uses of the Net today are diverse and increasing on an almost daily basis as more and more people realise its potential and scramble to take advantage. Academic research is a popular one as information on literally every topic under the sun can be readily accessed.

Gamers use the Net in gaming networks to compete against each other. Online businesses are now common. Many people now do their banking electronically, never seeing the inside of a bank. However probably the most popular use of the Net is for e-mail.

History

Like any monstrous entity, which it is now rapidly becoming, it all had to start somewhere and in this case it began in the USA in the middle of the Cold War. During the nuclear stand-off between the two super powers, the Americans decided it would be a good idea to research the development of a system of communication which would be capable of surviving a nuclear attack. Obviously normal lines of communication couldn't be relied upon, telephone lines would be down, radio stations destroyed etc. To this end they came up with the concept of a network that had no obvious beginning, middle or end. All parts of the proposed system would be accessible from anywhere within the system and yet at the same time retain their independence. No individual component could be assigned more importance than any other as this would then make it an obvious target for attack. Thus any part of a network could be destroyed without affecting the remaining parts.

The organisation set up for this purpose was called the *Advanced Research Projects Agency* and in 1969 the fruits of its labours were revealed. Called ARPANET, initially it wasn't much to write home about, consisting as it did, of a small network of computers, which was used mainly in the transfer of scientific research data. By 1972 it had grown to some 37 sites and its expansion to what we know today as the Internet, began in earnest.

In 1983, a military offshoot was developed, called MILNET, which saw more rigorous security procedures employed. The network continued to flourish and 1984 saw the arrival of a new network called NSFNET (National Science Foundation Network). This network used newer, faster computers and allowed users at any academic establishment to access its data. Meanwhile in the UK, computer systems at five universities were linked into a new network that rapidly expanded taking in more universities and academic institutions. This network was called JANET (Joint Academic Network).

In the 1980's all of these networks, together with similar systems developed in other countries, began to join forces to form a truly international network comprised of many smaller networks. In this way the Internet was born and it now began to grow rapidly as increasing numbers of organisations took advantage of the global means of communication it offered.

As it grew in size however, inherent problems began to manifest themselves. One of which was the different methods of communication used depending on what type of information was being accessed and from where it was being accessed.

The need for a standardised environment, which would allow anyone, anywhere, to gain access to any type of Internet information became clear. To this end researchers at CERN (European Centre for Nuclear Research), developed what was called the World Wide Web, a medium using electronic *pages* of text and images that resembled the format of a magazine and which could be linked together where relevant.

World Wide Web

So we come to the most popular and well known manifestation of the Internet, namely the World Wide Web. For most people it's a relatively new concept and is initially seen in much the same way as a child would see a new toy, something to be played with in order to explore its possibilities. The novelty factor out of the way though, they then begin to look at it in more practical terms to see what particular uses it might have for them. One of the first things they will realise is what a marvellous medium it is for communication, both on a personal level and for business purposes.

The concept of e-mail has been around for a long time now in office environments but the Web takes it into a different league, making possible instant communication anywhere in the world. For example you can communicate with relatives and friends in Australia or South Africa and at local call rates to boot.

One of the Web's most fascinating applications is to allow anyone to create their own web site. This gives any computer owner an effective means of publishing. Whatever ideas you have, you can present them to the world if you so desire, without the need for a printing press or publisher. What's more the Internet is truly free in the sense that no one can tell you what you can post and what you can't. Censorship on the Net is an alien concept, it just doesn't exist, although whether this is a good thing perhaps remains to be seen. The Web has already had a major impact in fields such as education, business and communications. As it continues to grow, more uses will become apparent and it's a brave man who will predict just how far it can go.

Internet Service Providers

Before you can gain access to this brave new world though, you will need to connect your computer to it. This will require a modem, which is needed to convert the analog signals of the network to the digital signals of your PC.

The next thing is to choose your Internet Service Provider (ISP) and the method of connection you want. These two factors will be determined by your perceived use of the Net. An ISP provides what is basically the interface between you and the network. It will have any number of modems all directly connected to the Net and will allow you to use one of these modems if you subscribe to their service.

 Online ISPs also provide their own channels. These include sport, finance, shopping and entertainment. These ISPs are a good option for people worrying about their children accessing unsuitable material on the Net.

ISPs come in two types. The more traditional ISP is what is known as an Online Service Provider, a typical example being America Online (AOL). These ISPs don't just restrict themselves to providing the basic connection, they will provide you with other services once you are hooked up. One of the main advantages provided by these ISPs is ease of connection. All you have to do is open the set-up program, provide a few details and in literally a few minutes you are online and ready to go. This will obviously appeal to those who like an easy life, as they won't have to worry about the technicalities of the procedure. You will get good quality and reliable connections and a wealth of proprietary content, quite separate from the contents of the Web itself. This is generally family based stuff and covers a wide range of subjects such as travel, entertainment and education. Very popular features are chat areas, which allow you to communicate with people who share your interests. These ISPs provide extremely good service and customer relations and are, for these reasons, very popular. Other well known ISPs of this genre are LineOne, CompuServe (now known as CSi) and the Microsoft Network (MSN). The drawback with them is that they are usually more expensive.

The other type of ISP provides a more basic, no-frills service. There are well over 200 of them in the UK alone which makes choosing one somewhat of a dilemma. As with mobile phone companies they delight in offering tortuously complicated deals although recent trends have been to do away with up front charges altogether. The most well known example of this is *Freeserve*, an ISP launched at the beginning of 1999, which provided completely free access to the Net (telephone charges excluded). The emergence of Freeserve really set the ball rolling and within months free ISPs were springing up all over the place. Some of them went even further than Freeserve and provided free telephone calls as well, although these were usually only available in the early hours of the morning.

It all sounds wonderful and on the face of it, it would certainly seem to simplify matters when it comes to choosing an ISP. What's there to think about if one ISP is offering a completely free service and the other is asking you to pay for it? Sign me up now free ISP!

 When choosing an ISP remember there's more to consider than just the issue of charges. Will they be able to provide you with consistently reliable connections? Also, should you encounter problems do they provide good customer support?

The reality however is somewhat different and, if anything, has complicated the situation even more. For a start just how free are these so-called free ISPs? They're certainly not in business for the fun of it and you'd be naive to think otherwise. Free ISPs make their money in several ways, of which the most simple is taking a cut from the cost of your telephone connection when online. The next thing you'll notice is that you're having to literally pick your way round the constant hoards of advertisements that confront you at every turn. Another way is to set up deals with online shops, which will pay the ISP a commission on everything you buy from them. Some of these ISPs are subsidiaries of major companies who are using the Internet as a means of raising awareness of their brand name.

None of this though, alters the fact that they are still providing an Internet connection that does not require people to cough up for it, as long as they are prepared to put up with the never ending ads. People being what they are, always on the lookout for a good deal, have been signing up in droves with these ISPs and this has highlighted a major shortcoming with many of them.

In their frenzied haste to jump aboard the advertising bandwagon, they simply haven't taken the time to set up the service properly. This has resulted in them being vastly over subscribed and they simply cannot cope with the level of business they are attracting.

Thousands of people are now finding that their Internet connections are at best, tenuous, at worst, simply non-existent. Even worse is the attitude of some of these companies. Irate customers ringing to see what is going on are met with phones permanently off the hook while letters are routinely ignored.

The message here is that things are not always what they seem. If an offer seems too good to be true, then it usually is. Some good is coming out of all this though. In an effort to hang on to their customers, the older established ISPs and Online Providers have had to cut their monthly charges. Whereas in the past they really weren't that cheap, they are now beginning to look a much more attractive option.

Quite apart from the cost of ISPs there are, however, other considerations which you should take into account when choosing your provider. One very important factor is their *ratio of modems to users* and the speed of these modems. For instance, a provider might have one modem for every thirty customers. This might be fine for weekday calls but weekends could be a different matter. If you try connecting up on Saturday evening, you will find you are competing with numerous others, all taking advantage of the low weekend phone rates. This could well result in you having to make several attempts before you can get through. Also the speed of the connection is quite likely to be snail pace as the overloaded system struggles to cope. Establish the speed of the modems that the ISP uses. You can have the fastest modem in the world but your data transfer speed will only ever be as fast as the server's modem allows. The consequence of this is that you will spend longer online to complete any given task and so incur unnecessarily high phone costs.

Types of Connection

Irrespective of the ISP you end up with, you will need some means of connecting your modem to their modem. Modern day technology allows you a choice of two ways to do this. Firstly we have the telephone system, which is the most commonly used for the simple reason that it's the one we all already have. There are problems with telephone lines though, exacerbated by the burgeoning use of the Net. When the telegraphic system was originally designed, it was intended to carry analog signals suitable for the transmission of sound. For computers to be able to use this medium, their digital output has to be first converted into sound, transmitted and then reconverted back into digital data. Now while the frequency range (bandwidth) of telephone lines is quite suitable for sound transmission, it is far from ideal for digital data that would benefit greatly from wider bandwidths. In the past this wasn't the problem that it is today for the simple reason that there wasn't all that much Internet traffic about. Now though, Internet usage has increased vastly, to the point where the telephone system is beginning to struggle coping with it.

Never forget that every minute spent online means a higher phone bill. If possible restrict your use to evenings and weekends when call rates are considerably reduced.

This brings us to the second method of Internet connection, namely ISDN, which stands for *Integrated Services Digital Network*. This system uses fibre-optic cable, which is fully capable of transmitting data in digital form. What's more it has the necessary bandwidth to cope with the amount of data now being generated by the use of the Net. The great advantage of this is that of speed. ISDN permits the transfer of data at speeds that are almost a rival for hard disk drives. Also, as it's a permanent connection and does not require modems, the connection speed is typically only two or three seconds. ISDN has been available for many years in this country but it is only in the last two or three that its use has become more prevalent, due mainly to its high cost. More recently though, the option of installing an ISDN connection has become more feasible as competition has forced prices down to a more realistic level. For the average Internet user though, who has no real need of the reliability and speed that ISDN offers, it continues to be an unviable option, as it is far from cheap.

A more recent development is Asymmetrical Digital Subscriber Line (ADSL), although the basic technology isn't new. With this system data is sent through two different channels, one for upstream (uploading) and one for downstream (downloading). It's called asymmetrical because the data in the two channels is transmitted at different speeds. Downstream it's sent at speeds of up 8Mb per second while the upstream channel is about 1Mb per second. The reason for this is that most Internet users spend more time downloading than they do uploading, so this makes for a more efficient use of the system's resources. ASDL works on telephone lines and thus requires two modems, one on each side of the connection. This technology is already available to users in the USA but it's unlikely to be available in the UK for a while yet. When it is eventually made available here, the speeds offered are unlikely to be anything near the figures mentioned above. The reason for this is basically a trade off between performance and price. Anticipated speeds are more likely to download at around 1.5Mbps and upload at around 0.5Mbps, still 25 times faster than presently available.

Other developments in the pipeline are cable modem systems offering potentially huge increases in performance. Another interesting theory involves using electricity power lines with access being gained through mains sockets.

Internet Software

Although you should be aware of the distinction between the two types of Internet software, both types may be set up automatically at the same time by some service providers' installation packages.

Internet software falls into two categories. Firstly, you need a program with which to set up your connection with your chosen ISP, and secondly you need software that will act as an interface between you and the Web itself. All computers on the Internet communicate with each other through a common digital language or set of standards, known as TCP/IP (Transmission Control Protocol/Internet Protocol). The connection software used by your PC is called a *winsock* and uses TCP/IP to control how your computer communicates with your modem and how the modem communicates with your ISP's modem. This will require the user to enter some settings before he will be able to log on to the Net for the first time. From this point on the procedure will be automatic. Windows is supplied with a built in winsock but your ISP will probably provide you with all the software necessary in the form of a CD. The connection program will also store information about you, such as your user name, password and account details and will automatically pass these to the ISP each time you log on.

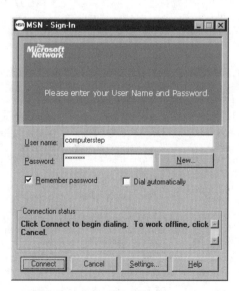

Web Browsers

Once actually online you need some means of seeing what's there. This interface is known as a web browser, which can be considered as a *portal* or *window.* What you'll see is much the same as a normal 'Windows' window, with a toolbar running along the top. You will also find an e-mail application here. The box beginning with http// is your entry to the Web. Here you type the web address of the site you are looking for. Then press Enter and within a few seconds the requested site will open up in the browser.

The two main browsers that the Internet user is likely to come across are *Netscape Communicator* and Microsoft's *Internet Explorer.* Netscape were the developers of the original Navigator, which for a long time was the major web browser as there were no other comparable browsers around. However when Microsoft started taking an interest in the Net, they came out with their own version that was called Internet Explorer. As this browser was being shipped with all versions of Windows, it wasn't long before virtually all PCs had Internet Explorer installed as standard. As it was already there on their system most people didn't bother looking any further, with the predictable result that

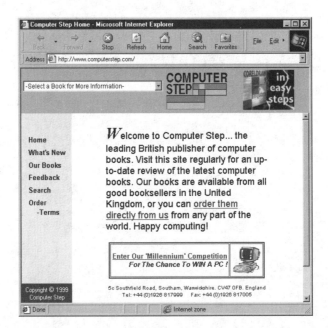

Netscape's Communicator was given the proverbial 'elbow'. Internet Explorer now rules the roost. It's lean, mean and completely free. It couldn't fail really.

With the introduction of Windows 98, Microsoft took the concept a stage further by integrating Internet Explorer within the Windows operating system, whereby any open window can be configured to look and act as a browser. This makes it possible to access any web site directly from a window simply by typing in its address.

Web Sites

A web site is basically an electronic book, in the case of the larger sites. Smaller sites can be thought of as magazines while little sites might be no more than a single page. The information they contain is entirely at the whim of the site's creator and will range from the extremely useful, to the mundane, to the fatuous and right down to the offensive.

The home page is the first page you will see. It contains general details of what the site has to offer, much as the table of contents in a book will. As you study the home page one of the first things you'll notice is what's known as a *hyperlink,* which is a text phrase or a graphic. Clicking on one of these takes you to a new page that will contain material related to that in the home page. These hyperlinks are extremely useful things and can save a tremendous amount of time. For example let's say you are doing a thesis on the D-Day landings in World War II and you manage to navigate your way to a suitable site. The problem you might now have is being faced with *too* much information, as the World War II was an enormous event in world history and a full coverage will by necessity, involve many many articles. You don't want to have to plough through the Russian campaign or the ins and outs of the Battle of Britain, all you need are details concerning the D-Day Landings. This is where hyperlinks come in. A well designed site will have plenty of these things and for this very purpose. The first links you see might not lead directly to the article you want but they will quickly narrow down the search, much as a table of contents in a book will.

Having found the desired article, you might then find more hyperlinks in the article itself that lead to other related articles. In this way you can be sure you have seen all the site has to offer without having to trawl through page after page to make sure you haven't missed anything relevant. Hyperlinks can lead to pages in the same site or to completely different sites on the other side of the world. As an example of this, your article on the D-Day Landings might contain a link to a site in France that specialises in the role of the French Underground during the landings. Using the hyperlink you can simply jump from one site to the other without having to go through the rigmarole of leaving the first site, finding the address of the second and then typing it in to make the new connection.

The range of web sites you will find today cover literally every field of human endeavour, from serious topics such as business, education, science and academic study, right down to the frivolous such as games, cartoons and general nonsense. Many sites provide genuinely useful and worthwhile information while others make you wonder why its creator bothered. Much of what you'll find on the Net is absolute rubbish serving only as an outlet for its author's prejudices and fantasies. Many sites are downright offensive in nature while others provide much needed light heartedness and humour.

Search Engines

There are now generally reckoned to be something approaching 100 million web sites floating about in the ether, with the number growing all the time. This is fine if all you want to do is browse about and see what comes up. You won't run out of material that's for sure. But if you are looking for something specific it can make life difficult.

To this end we have what are known as search engines, which are essentially huge databases containing the addresses and details of hundreds of thousands, if not millions, of web sites. The ways that sites get listed on these search engines vary, with the most obvious being the site's author registering his site with a particular search engine.

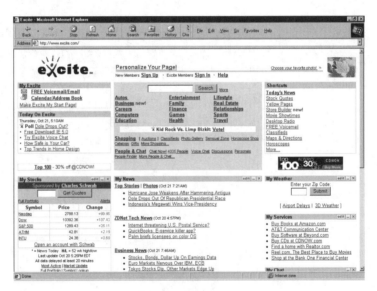

Many search engines run regular programs fetchingly entitled *Web Crawlers*, or *Spiders*, to gather information and increase their databases. These crawlers trawl the Net by following any hyperlinks they encounter and then send the details back to the search engines to be indexed. Some are programmed to follow every link they come across while others will only track certain types of link. Back at the search engine, its software analyses the site's content and then indexes the site accordingly.

When someone decides, for example, that he wants information on George Washington, he'll visit a search engine's web site and in the keyword box type in George Washington. The search engine will respond by displaying a list of all the sites it knows about that are related to the entered keyword. Good engines employ the Boolean Operator system to narrow the search.

The list displayed by the search engine will often contain the first four or five sentences of the site's documents and will also put the sites in an order of ranking that it thinks will be most relevant. Each of the sites listed will have a hyperlink that you just have to click in order to visit them.

Given the incredible number of web sites, many of which are closing at the same time that new ones are opening, it is clearly an impossible task to keep tabs on them all. Even the biggest search engines will only list a small percentage of the available sites at any one time. As a matter of interest, search engines don't exist just to make life easy for the masses. Thanks to the massive amount of visits (hits) they receive, they are wonderful platforms for advertisers in just the same way as the free ISPs are, and the revenue they make in this way is enormous.

Some of the main search engines you can try are:

http://www.altavista.com

http://www.excite.com

http://www.lycos

http://www.infoseek.com

http://www.webcrawler.com

http://www.askjeeves.com

Surfing the Web

One of the most useful applications of the Web is to allow you to download data. Be aware though that because of the inherent slowness of the telephone system, downloading large files or programs can take a long time.

The whole point of the Web was to make access to limitless amounts of information as easy and simple as possible. With this in mind it can't be denied that the way the system has been structured and organised, works extremely well. In fact as far as the user is concerned, it really couldn't be simpler, all you have to do is point at something, click a button, and hey presto, it appears before you. The only real fly in the ointment, is something the Web's creators could never have visualised – its massive proportions. This of course makes looking for something specific a potential nightmare. For the moment though there seems to be no real answer to this so for the time being we'll just have to accept this limitation.

The view of the Web described so far in this chapter is somewhat limited. It is not just a very sophisticated electronic book or magazine. There are types of media that cannot begin to be described in terms of magazine pages. For instance, on a seemingly ordinary looking web page you may come across a link to a site containing a Virtual Reality environment, a term that has been much bandied about in recent years. This concept concerns the creation of virtual electronic worlds through which you may 'travel', using a computer screen. The idea is that you become totally immersed in the experience and can interact with what's going on. Many ambitious claims have been made for Virtual Reality, such as allowing people on other sides of the world to interact in a virtual environment as if they were physically in the same room. For example medical students could practise operating on virtual 'patients' before being let loose on the real thing. However the virtual environments currently available on the Web do not really live up to what has been claimed for them.

You will also find links to files containing video or audio clips – simply click to open them. Some are designed to be played while you are viewing the site, which will require the appropriate software to be on your system. For example many sound recordings available on the Web are stored in *RealAudio* format. These allow you to play the recording whilst they are being downloaded. To play them you need a RealAudio player and the term used to describe files accessed in this way is *Streaming Video or Audio*.

As already explained on page 87, computers have a problem with the bandwidth limitations placed on them by the telephone line system. This problem is intensified when using sound or video files because of their enormous size. The traditional method used in getting round this problem, compression, is still not adequate. So by necessity sound and video from the Net is delivered with much reduced quality, i.e. the number of frames in a video clip is much reduced as is its size and length. The introduction of streaming technology further opened up the Net's potential uses. Now it's possible to listen to a live radio station from anywhere in the world, listen to concerts or even watch live television broadcasts.

To access a web site you must have its address, just as you would need a house address before you could find it. The address of any Internet site is known as a Uniform Resource Locator (URL). While the postal addresses that we are more familiar with begin with the specifics and end with the more general, URLs work in a more convoluted way.

Consider the following web address:

http://www.computerstep.com/1840780452.html

   1   2   3   4   5   6

Part 1, http://, stands for *hypertext transfer protocol* and defines the type of service that is available at this address.

Parts 2–4 comprise the *domain* name, whose conventions are also used by other non-web sites on the Net. Part 2, WWW, as you might expect, stands for World Wide Web, and tells the browser that the site in question is a web site.

Part 3, computerstep, is the name of the site, equivalent to the house number or name in a postal address. This particular address is that of Computer Step's web site.

Part 4, .com, denotes what sort of organisation is using the site. In this case, com, stands for commercial. The number of different types of organisation is relatively small, though the code used depends on whether the site is international, or specific to a particular country.

The following table shows you some of the more common types of organisation:

Type of Organisation	UK Code	US/International Code
Academic	ac.uk	edu
Commercial	co.uk	com
Government	gov.uk (or govt.uk)	gov
Internet	net.uk	net
Non-profit	org.uk	org
Schools	sch.uk	sch

At part 5, the URL begins to get more specific again. In our example, part 5 represents the name of the HTML file containing information on this book. However, many domains are further divided into subdirectories, just as your hard drive is. A URL you see might include directions, through several nested subdirectories, at the end of which there may or may not be a file name. If there isn't one then the web server will automatically send your browser the default starting page for that location, often called index.html.

The fact that all this works as well as it does is little short of a miracle when you consider that even the most basic communication is separated into different parcels which are then sent over thousands of miles of telephone lines, satellite link-ups and cable systems. Along the way they are coded, decoded, compressed and decompressed, lost and found, translated and retranslated. The individual parcels might not even take the same route and only get reunited towards the end of the link. Perhaps even more amazing is the fact that no one's actually in charge of the thing. The Internet is a free entity, owned by nobody and beholden to nobody.

HTML and Web Page Design

See HTML and Web Page Design in easy steps to help you create your own web site.

Having looked at a few web sites with all their fancy graphics and hyperlinks leading to other pages or related sites, you could be forgiven for assuming that the creation of such sites is not something to be attempted by the amateur. This is however, far from the case. Like everything else related to the Web, page design is intended to be a simple process.

All web pages are put together using a very simple language known as *Hypertext Markup Language (HTML)*. This language is basically comprised of a limited number of simple codes that are inserted into the text you write. These codes instruct your browser to apply various effects to the text, i.e. underlining, or to place a picture or hyperlink at a certain place in the page. You do not need any special programming tools to write HTML, you can create a web page using a simple text editor like Wordpad, or by using a specially designed template in a word processor such as Microsoft Word.

HTML codes are extremely similar to the type of codes used on the older DOS word processors before the arrival of Windows. For example the HTML code to turn italics on is: <I>, while </I> turns the italics off.

All HTML codes work in this way. A hyperlink is created by inserting a special code followed by the web address of the page, while a picture is also inserted in the same manner.

Virtual Servers

Once your web page has been created, you need somewhere to put it so that others can see it. If it is only a personal home page, you can take advantage of the small amount of free web space that will be provided by your ISP. The address for your site would then be a subdirectory of the ISP's site, a fact which would be obvious to anyone accessing it.

However there may be various reasons why you would not want anyone to be aware of this fact. For example if you are creating a business site, you might want to create the impression that you are running a major concern, something that would be unlikely if you are merely a sub-part of someone else's site.

One way of doing this is to set up your own server. This however requires an ISDN connection or leased telephone line, plus ancillary equipment. This will prove to be an expensive operation both to set up and to maintain. You might find that the level of business the site generates does not warrant the expense involved.

A cheaper option is to set up as a *virtual server*. Your pages will still be located in a subdirectory of a true server, however your address will appear as though you are a server in your own right. For example, instead of a URL like this:

http://www.serviceprovider.co.uk/mywebsite/

it will read like this:

http://www.mywebsite.co.uk

Most good service providers will provide this facility, at a price not surprisingly, and there are also companies who specialise in setting up virtual servers.

Whenever a server, true or virtual, is set up, it must have a domain name that is unique. To ensure that the name you have chosen is not already in use, you must register it with the relevant authority. Domain names ending in *co.uk*, should be registered with Nominet (http://www.nic.uk). Names ending in *.com*, are the province of the American organisation Internic (http:www.internic.net).

You aren't restricted to using a *co.uk* domain just because you are located in the UK – you're free to choose a *.com* domain if you want to give your site an international flavour.

E-mail

Despite all the many and varied uses of the Internet, the single main reason that most people get hooked up is to explore the world of e-mail. As a result the stuff is everywhere. In office environments it has all but replaced the old fashioned memo and indeed why wouldn't it? It's quick, cheap and inexpensive. In this application it really has replaced paper.

These same advantages also apply on a more global scale and indeed are even more applicable. For example in terms of cost there's not much between a memo and its electronic equivalent. However a lengthy document sent abroad by e-mail will be much cheaper than if sent by post. Plus of course it will arrive within minutes as opposed to maybe a week. It's also still not unknown for a letter sent by post to simply disappear. This problem rarely, if ever, occurs with an e-mail.

E-mails also compare favourably with communication methods such as telephone calls and faxes. For a telephone connection to be successful both parties must be available, if the party called is not in, then the exercise has been a waste of time. They might of course have an answering machine hooked up, in which case you can leave your message. But as we all know, being suddenly confronted with an impersonal answering machine can be a somewhat off-putting experience and you often come away wishing you could erase what you've just said and start again.

There are still some things that e-mail cannot do as well as a letter or telephone call, and these are realised mostly in the realm of personal, as opposed to business, communication. You can't hear the voice of your loved ones via e-mail; equally, you miss out on the expressiveness of someone's handwriting, and you can't doodle in the margin (though you can send encoded pictures). These, though, are minor gripes, and do nothing to hold back e-mail as the most effective means of communication for many purposes.

E-mail allows you to formulate the message clearly and concisely before it's sent. With regard to fax machines, these are not the most reliable and efficient means of communication. Very often the quality is invariably poorer than the original. Messages sent via e-mail do not suffer from this problem as they are composed entirely of digital characters which are unaffected by the vagaries of the telephone line.

Thus e-mail takes the best features of the written letter, the telephone call and the fax, and for most purposes, transcends them. Messages communicated by telephone are spontaneous, you speak the words as they come into your head and so are prone to mistakes or omissions. It's also easy to be distracted while on the phone by some external event, someone knocking on the door for example. By the time you've got back on the phone you've probably lost the thread of what you were saying. For these reasons it's all too easy to end up with an unsatisfactory phone call with things left unsaid. You could of course make another call, but in practise how many of us do? Particularly if it's an overseas call. The e-mail allows you to get all the pertinent details right before the link is made.

Messages sent by e-mail tend to be more fun and light-hearted. The usual rules of formality, particularly with business correspondence, are invariably relaxed. Little witticisms can be added, which in a formal document would come across as frivolous.

So how do you do all this? How do you actually write an e-mail and once you've sent it off, how does it get to its destination? Firstly you need an e-mail program. Most PCs these days will be supplied with several and all you have to do is decide which one is most likely to suit you. They are all much of a muchness, providing a main window for composing your message, various folders such as an *inbox, outbox, messages sent* and *messages deleted*. There will be an address book in which to keep details of your favourite e-mail addresses.

...cont'd

A point worth making here is that it's not necessary to be online, i.e. spending money, to write or read an e-mail. The idea is that you compose your message, taking all the time you need, before logging on. Then all you need do is click *send*. At the same time you can check for incoming mail.

When writing an e-mail, just as with writing a letter, there are a few basic rules to follow. There are several items of information that need to be included with an e-mail before it can be sent. Since you don't need an envelope, all this information is attached to the top of the message, as a header. Your e-mail program will represent this header as usually three boxes to be filled in. This will look as follows;

To	Cc
From	Bcc
Subject	Attachments

The *To* box is where you enter the e-mail address and it can either be typed in manually or selected from the address book, assuming it's in there. A typical e-mail address will look as follows: john@aol.co.uk

The last two parts will be familiar assuming you have read pages 96–97, and tell us that the address is located at a commercial company in the UK. Aol is the name of the service provider, in this case America Online. Everything to the left of the @ symbol distinguishes the holder of this e-mail address from all the other customers of the ISP. Most ISPs will allow you to choose this part of the address yourself, most people use their own name. Some however assign user identification codes to each of their customers.

You won't have to enter your name and address in the *From* box, as once your details are entered in the initial setting up procedure, this is done automatically. Your full name usually appears in front of your address and will appear on the message the recipient receives, but it's not a vital part of the address and you can change it in the program settings.

In the *Subject* box you can enter some very brief information regarding the subject matter of the message. This will give the recipient some idea what the message concerns and is useful if the correspondence evolves into a string of related messages and replies.

Cc stands for carbon copies. In this box you can enter the address of anyone else you want to send the message to. Your service provider's mail system will then automatically forward a copy of the message to the address or addresses specified. This saves you sending the message a number of times. The information in this box will be available to all the recipients. If however you don't want people to know who else has received the same message, enter the addresses in the box labelled *Bcc* (Blind carbon copies).

Attachments is another optional category that allows you to send any file in your PC with the message. These could be anything from entire programs to graphics files. Strictly speaking e-mail can only contain ASCII text, and so in order for you to be able to send a binary file it must be encoded, i.e. all its zeroes and ones must be converted into letters, numbers and symbols using a system that will allow them to be converted back into their original form by your recipient. The e-mail program will usually handle this procedure for you, all you have to do is specify which files you want encoding. However there are several different formats of encoding, e.g. Uuencode and MIME, and you might have trouble if you encode a file in a format that is not recognised by your recipient's e-mail program. For this reason it's a good idea to check that you are both using a commonly recognisable format.

You can read any normal ASCII e-mail you might receive regardless of who it's from, but be very wary of attached files if it's from a stranger. This is how viruses are transmitted on the Internet. The advice here is categoric – do **not** open any files attached to an e-mail if the sender is unknown to you. If you do, you could find yourself with something very nasty indeed.

How Does Your Message Get There?

Assuming the presence of a graphics attachment, your e-mail program (client), first encodes it into ASCII text and may also compress it to speed up the transmission. The e-mail program establishes contact with the ISP's computer and then connects to a program known as an *SMTP server (Simple Mail Transfer Protocol)*. The ISP acknowledges the contact at which point the client advises the server that it has a message waiting to be sent. The ISP responds by telling the client to send the message or to wait until later (assuming it's busy). After transmission the client requests confirmation of receipt, which is granted assuming the message has been received. The SMTP server now contacts another software program, known as a *Domain Name Server* and requests the best available route. After checking, the domain name server will pass on the requested information.

The SMTP now sends the message. During its journey the message will be directed by Internet *Routers*, that determine which route is the best currently available. Depending on its destination the message may also pass through *Gateways*, which allow different types of computer systems to be interlinked. When the e-mail finally arrives at the addressees SMTP server, it is transferred to another server called a *POP (Post Office Protocol)* server. Here the message will be held. When the recipient next logs on to the system he will be informed he has mail waiting. The POP server retrieves the message and sends it to the recipient's e-mail program, where it's decompressed and then displayed for viewing.

Newsgroups

When deciding which service provider to sign up with, ask them about the number of newsgroups they provide with their Usenet feed; avoid service providers who offer a small number of newsgroups. Just because a newsgroup exists doesn't mean you will be able to access it via your service provider's newsfeed.

The term *newsgroups* is something of a misnomer, since the vast majority of them deal with chat or topical discussion, not news. Newsgroups are organised in groups interested in specific subjects. Information is posted on *bulletin boards* that are accessible to anyone with the appropriate newsgroup access.

If for example you have a sudden desire to catch up on what's happening in the world of astrophysics, all you have to do is visit the bulletin board to see the latest developments. Doing things in this way means that users don't have endless streams of e-mails waiting to be read.

One particular advantage of Usenet is that its newsgroups are organised by subject type, not by the location at which they are managed – so it's much easier to find the groups of interest to you. There are many Usenet categories, though most of them fall within one of the following categories:

comp	Computing
sci	Science
rec	Recreation
soc	Social
misc	Miscellaneous
alt	Alternative

The subject matter of most of these is fairly obvious, with the exception perhaps of *misc* and *alt*. The reason for the existence of these two is mostly historical. The first five categories were established when Usenet was first conceived and any topic that couldn't be placed within one of these was assigned to misc. That was several years ago and now the misc group itself has its standard categories. As most subjects can now be placed within one of the first five groups, any new topics that come along tend to be somewhat arcane in nature. These are immediately classified under the *alt* heading.

In order to read any messages posted to a newsgroup, you need a service provider who will provide a Usenet feed and a Usenet newsreader program. Free Agent is a popular newsreader program and can be downloaded from http://www.forteinc.com/forte/.

 If you intend to make much use of Usenet, you will probably find that a dedicated newsreader program provides the best range of facilities. However, Outlook Express, the communications program bundled with Internet Explorer, has a perfectly adequate newsgroup-reading facility.

While mailing lists and Usenet newsgroups can provide very informative and entertaining forums for discussion on a wide range of subjects, they are susceptible to a particularly annoying Internet phenomena known as *spamming*. E-mail users can also be subjected to this irritation. Spamming or spam mail, as it's called, is the indiscriminate posting of the same message to a large number of e-mail addresses. This practice is usually the work of businesses attempting to use the Internet as an advertising medium. Spamming is the Internet equivalent of postal mailshots.

Given the potential of the Internet for this purpose, the practice is not actually as common as you might expect. One reason for this is that computer users seem to react more strongly to spam mail than they would to a mailshot, and several thousand irate e-mails sent back to a spammer can have strange effects on his computer system.

Internet Security

To many people, the best thing about the Internet is the fact that in its anarchic way, it does away with censorship and media control. To those living in the Western nations, this concept is not particularly novel but consider the eye opener it must be to those living in more repressive Communist regimes. Even Western governments are not averse to 'doctoring' the way certain events are presented to the people if they think they can get away with it. In a democratic society this is never a good thing and the Net provides a way for a civically minded citizen to 'spill the beans' about any political shenanigans that are going on.

For all the freedom it offers though, the Internet can also provide the more unscrupulous amongst us with an avenue through which to carry out their dirty deeds. These can range from having our inboxes swamped with unwanted and sometimes offensive e-mail, to credit card fraud or having our systems infected with malicious viruses.

 Be wary of giving out credit card details on the Net unless you are dealing with a reputable company.

E-mails are susceptible to a nasty form of interference often called 'being nosey'. An electronic message sent via the Net can take a tortuous route before finally arriving at its destination. Along the way it will pass through any number of computers, at any of which your message can be read. However most of the stuff you send by e-mail will be of the postcard variety, which is similarly prone to nosey parkerism. As there's nothing we can do to stop our post cards being read, we don't write anything on them that could have any possible value to someone else. For most people this will be the solution used to protect their e-mails. If it's not worth reading, then it won't get read.

To some people however this attitude might seem a bit flippant and so they'll be pleased to know there is a way to keep prying eyes out of their mail, or rather to prevent it making any sense to them. All that's needed is a piece of software known as an encryption program. As the use of e-mail has increased, so too has concern over this issue of privacy. In response, there are now several proprietary programs that will scramble your data before it leaves your browser. For this to work however, the recipient has to have the same software with which to unscramble the message.

A more serious problem that has reared its ugly head with the advent of online shopping, is that of credit card fraud. One of the biggest attractions to people of online shopping is not just its convenience but also its speed. Just select your item, pay for it and within 24 hours you should have received it (that's the theory anyway). The trouble is for this to happen you need to pay electronically, i.e. by credit card.

Credit card fraud is remarkably easy. All you need is someone's name and card number. Fortunately though, as credit card facilities are so important to the commercial side of the Web, serious efforts have gone into making them a safe way of paying for your goods. In the same way as e-mails can be encrypted so can credit card details and other sensitive information. The interception of your data while being transmitted isn't the only way it can be accessed. If you are using your credit card to pay for something, then for a limited period at least, your details will be sitting in someone's computerised database. Here they will be a sitting target for a computer hacker.

There's no need to worry though. To guard against this possibility we have something known as a *firewall*. This system is probably the most widely used method of protecting confidential data on the Net from unauthorised access. The idea is that computers holding sensitive information are isolated from the Net, while still being capable of receiving consumer information from it. The server computer, which does all the communication with outside users, acts as a 'middle man', receiving any confidential information, without storing it and then passing it on, via an internal link, to the organisation's main computers. These main computers have no other link to the Net and are programmed to only respond to the server's computer. In theory this system is foolproof, whether or not it actually is remains to be seen. At the moment you have as much chance of being ripped off by using your credit card at a local restaurant as on the Net.

Netiquette

As with any social institution, there are rules regarding what is and is not acceptable behaviour on the Internet. If you're simply browsing a Web page, these rules don't really come into play. However, a good deal of the traffic on the Internet involves interpersonal communication, as with e-mail and newsgroups, and it is here that you should be aware of the complex matter of *netiquette*. Communication on the Internet differs from normal social interaction, in that the medium is largely textual, and so the nuances of voice and facial expression that might help to clarify someone's precise meaning and intentions in a face-to-face situation, or a telephone conversation, are lost. Another problem arises from the fact that Internet communication is spontaneous, though its effects are potentially permanent. For example, a rash, rude remark made in a vocal conversation can quickly be glossed over and forgotten by both parties; while an insult sent in the heat of anger to a Usenet newsgroup, almost as spontaneously, can be filed on someone's hard drive and kept indefinitely.

In order to prevent such electronic *faux pas*, you should keep in mind that, in a medium devoid of smirks, tongues-in-cheek, and comical tones of voice, any jocular or sarcastic remark you make on the Internet might be taken in a completely unintended way, as offensive, aggressive or just plain stupid. In an attempt to remedy this kind of problem, the society of the nascent Internet, composed largely of computer programmers, developed a system of abbreviations and *emoticons*, which were intended to express their true emotions.

If you study any newsgroup or Internet Relay Chat discussion for a short while, you are likely to find the conversation peppered with seemingly meaningless sequences of letters, like "ROFL", "IMHO" and "FWIW". These in fact stand respectively for "rolling on the floor laughing", "in my humble opinion" and "for what it's worth". They are probably used as much to make initiates feel smugly superior, and to exclude bewildered new users ("newbies"), as to save typing time, and they clearly can't convey any emotion as subtly for instance as a well-judged smile. However, they are used quite often in certain areas of the Internet, so if you encounter them it would be worth your while to understand at least the most popular ones, if only to show to other, more seasoned users that you're not completely green. Some other abbreviations you might see are:

BBL	Be back later
BTW	By the way
FYI	For your information
GAL	Get a life
HTH	Hope this helps
IOW	In other words
IYSWIM	If you see what I mean
LOL	Laughing out loud
OIC	Oh I see
OTOH	On the other hand
PMFBI	Pardon me for butting in

The other type of emotional short-hand, emoticons, are often also known as *smileys*. This is because the first emoticon was a textual representation of a smiling face, as follows: :-)   (twist the book clockwise by 90° if you can't make it out). This is normally used to show that the writer is not entirely serious about what he or she has just said, and that perhaps the reader should search for an element of irony in the message before responding angrily. As such, emoticons can be a very useful tool, but some people tend to go a little overboard with them. Here are some others you might want to try, of varying advisability:

:-(	Sad face
;-)	Wink
:-D	Laughing
:-o	Shock
:-p	Tongue stuck out
:-&	Tongue-tied
}:>	Devil
o:-)	Angel

Despite these safeguards against Internet misunderstandings, things can go dreadfully awry, especially if someone is being wilfully malicious or arrogantly inconsiderate. An example of this is *trolling*, often seen in newsgroups. A troll is a deliberate attempt by someone posting a message to provoke a flood of indignant replies by people incensed that someone could be so controversial or rude. In fishing terms, *to troll* is to cast out a baited line from a boat and draw it back through the water in the hope of attracting fish as it passes. This special brand of Internet trolling might then sound a little masochistic, but the intention of the troller is probably to give himself a feeling of omnipotence and superiority in the knowledge that tens, perhaps hundreds, of people are wasting their time trying to browbeat someone into moral submission over a point that he probably doesn't care a thing about.

This flood of angry replies provoked by the troller, or by someone unwittingly making an inappropriate remark, is known as *flaming*. A *flame* is not a level-headed statement of one's difference of opinion, but a personal attack on someone, often sent angrily and spontaneously. Again, this may be the result of some misunderstanding of intention, owing to the lack of extraverbal cues available on the Internet. More often than not, though, people may simply be spoiling for an argument. A *flame war* is the phenomenon that occurs when someone who has been flamed does not admit defeat, but flames back. This may lead to counter-flames, and fresh flames from like-minded individuals who have been drawn into the argument. The various flaming parties may polarise, leading to a protracted flame war of several weeks, or even months, between two diametrically opposed groups. By this time the war has usually degenerated into gratuitous name-calling. Perhaps in years to come the development of new, effective emoticons might put an end to misunderstandings on the Internet, and hence eradicate this pointless fighting ;-).

Software

Every component of a computer system has a role to play and some are more important than others. Software falls into this category, as without it you may as well try and fly an aeroplane without any controls. You won't even get it off the ground, never mind fly anywhere. So it is with the computer. To be able to get it up and running and then do something useful with it, you need software. This chapter describes all the different types of software available today.

Covers

Chapter Four

Introduction

Computers are wonderful things, amazing in their complexity but they're stupid. You have to tell them to do something, otherwise they will just sit there staring blankly at you. You might have the most wonderfully specified PC that money can buy, complete with 21 inch monitor, laser printer, DVD, super charged graphics, not to mention the latest in digital cameras. You might even have gone to the lengths of setting aside a special room in the house to keep it all in.

Without software however, it will all be totally useless, you won't be able to do a thing with it. In order to bring that expensive collection of plastic and silicon to life, you need software and this comes in two main types, namely; system software and application software.

System software is the operating system, Windows in most cases. As we have already seen, system software controls the internal workings of the PC together with all the associated hardware peripherals, such as monitors, drives and modems.

Application software directs the computer to execute commands given by the user. It could be accurately described as including any application that processes data for a user.

At its most basic level software consists of a detailed plan or procedure, or more specifically, an unambiguous, ordered sequence of computational instructions necessary to achieve a particular end. This plan is written in the form of coded instructions and with large programs can run into thousands, even millions, of lines of code. When loaded into a PC the coded instructions inform the computer what is expected of it and then makes sure that its orders are carried out.

Types of Software

There are literally thousands of software applications for the PC on today's market just waiting for you to go and buy them. Many of them will be well written, useful programs that will help you to utilise your PC fully. Others will come in pretty boxes, promising the earth, but when you run them you will find that they are often worth less than the box they came in.

So how will you know which are the Aces and which are the Jokers? Where is the best place to buy and what do you need to look out for? Read on!

Although, as already stated, there are a vast number of programs out there in the shops, they can be broadly classified into various categories.

 A very useful source of software is the free CDs distributed by the computer magazines. These range from demos of the latest games to full versions of some software packages.

- Word Processors
- Spreadsheets
- Databases
- Personal Organisers
- Office Suites
- Accounts/Finance
- Utilities
- Graphics
- Desktop Publishing
- Multimedia
- Education
- Reference
- Games
- Anti Virus
- Voice Recognition

Word Processor

One of the most useful applications you will ever load onto your PC will be a word processor. As with everything else these come in various standards from the most basic, an example being *Wordpad* supplied by Windows itself, to those such as Microsoft's Word.

These programs have almost rendered the old fashioned typewriter obsolete as they can do so very much more than just put letters onto paper.

Not everybody, of course, has the need for the wide range of options provided by the top end word processors and as such might not want to fork out for one of these. The aforementioned Wordpad, found under *Programs, Accessories,* is more than adequate for most purposes and its limited range of features is still head and shoulders above any typewriter.

The better word processors, of which Microsoft's Word reigns supreme, really have to be seen to be believed and offer an almost baffling array of functions. To begin with they offer you the choice of a number of templates such as letters, faxes and invoices which you can then customise to your own requirements and then save as a new template.

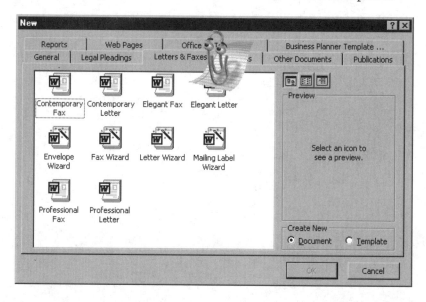

If you are running a business for example, you can quickly create a standard invoice form. You can of course design one yourself if you so choose. The various tools allow you to move selected blocks of text within a document or import text and graphics from other applications, set tabs, headings, footnotes, insert page numbers, set margins and numerous other things. You can create and customise your own toolbars from an almost endless list of commands. You can also connect to the Internet and download Web content straight into a document.

Other useful features include spelling and grammar checkers, a thesaurus, auto-save that allows you to automatically save your work at set periods and mail merge. This last feature enables you to combine two documents, a typical application of which would be to merge a list of names and addresses with a standard letter to create personalised letters.

You can also at a glance check the properties of a document such as the number of pages it contains, the number of paragraphs and even the exact number of words.

Password protection is another option offered and will enable you to keep prying eyes out of your documents.

All advanced word processors will automatically generate a table of contents and also an index complete with page numbers. All you have to do is specify the required words and the program does the rest.

All in all, they are wonderful pieces of software and well worth the money. Other top word processing packages include Lotus Wordpro and Corel's Wordperfect.

Spreadsheet

A spreadsheet is basically an advanced calculator that enables you to make calculations and store the results indefinitely. Any numerical problem, which can be presented in rows and columns, can be solved by a spreadsheet.

They allow greater flexibility than a calculator because you are not restricted to just numbers, you can also enter text and formulas. If need be all three can be combined.

With a spreadsheet, not only can you use its specialised formulas, you can also create your own. Also it will come with various functions such as: mathematical, trigonomic, logical, date, statistical and financial.

One great benefit of using a spreadsheet is to be able to perform **"what if"** analysis. For example, John Smith wants to arrange a suitable overdraft facility with his bank. Let us assume that purchases are 50% of sales and variable costs are 10% of sales. This information can easily be entered in a spreadsheet and derived figures will be calculated automatically, as shown here.

	A	B	C	D	E	F	G
1	John Smith – Cash Flow Jan to Jun 2000						
2							
3		Jan-00	Feb-00	Mar-00	Apr-00	May-00	Jun-00
4							
5	Opening Bank Balance	-£3,000	-£2,000	-£2,600	-£2,800	£200	£4,800
6							
7	Sales Receipts	£10,000	£6,000	£7,000	£15,000	£19,000	£24,000
8							
9	Purchase Payments	£5,000	£3,000	£3,500	£7,500	£9,500	£12,000
10	Variable Costs Payments	£1,000	£600	£700	£1,500	£1,900	£2,400
11	Fixed Costs Payments	£3,000	£3,000	£3,000	£3,000	£3,000	£3,000
12	Total Outflow	£9,000	£6,600	£7,200	£12,000	£14,400	£17,400
13							
14	Closing Bank Balance	-£2,000	-£2,600	-£2,800	£200	£4,800	£11,400

We can also see that John Smith needs to arrange an overdraft facility until April 2000. Now, what if, sales receipts in just the first month were to drop to £5000. By making this single change, as shown here, the spreadsheet will recalculate all related figures instantly, at the touch of a button. You can also see that the overdraft will be required for an additional month.

	A	B	C	D	E	F	G
1	John Smith – Cash Flow Jan to Jun 2000						
2							
3		Jan-00	Feb-00	Mar-00	Apr-00	May-00	Jun-00
4							
5	Opening Bank Balance	-£3,000	-£4,000	-£4,600	-£4,800	-£1,800	£2,800
6							
7	Sales Receipts	£5,000	£6,000	£7,000	£15,000	£19,000	£24,000
8							
9	Purchase Payments	£2,500	£3,000	£3,500	£7,500	£9,500	£12,000
10	Variable Costs Payments	£500	£600	£700	£1,500	£1,900	£2,400
11	Fixed Costs Payments	£3,000	£3,000	£3,000	£3,000	£3,000	£3,000
12	Total Outflow	£6,000	£6,600	£7,200	£12,000	£14,400	£17,400
13							
14	Closing Bank Balance	-£4,000	-£4,600	-£4,800	-£1,800	£2,800	£9,400

This is a very simple example to make the point. You can make it more realistic by incorprating bank interest, breakdown of expenses, breakdown of sales by product and so on. In brief, once you have raw data in a spreadsheet, you can have any number of scenarios, no matter how complex they might be. You can use a spreadsheet for repetitive accounting tasks or as a tool for management decision making.

Macros are very important for automating repetitive procedures within a spreadsheet. You can execute a macro representing several different keystrokes by simply pressing one function key. The use of macros can speed up your work and generally simplify things. Macros can also be used to customise a spreadsheet for specific applications.

A common saying is that a picture is as good as a thousand words and this truism can certainly apply to raw data. In spreadsheet applications a good graphic, such as a bar graph or piechart, can make all the difference when a complicated document comes to be analysed. Displaying data in a graphic format is easily possible with a spreadsheet.

Another way these applications can be used is to *link* various smaller spreadsheets which in themselves are easier to work with. When they are completed they can then all be linked to effectively form one huge spreadsheet.

Changing a value in one of the spreadsheets will automatically recalculate all related values in the others.

As an example of this, say you want to create a spreadsheet to monitor your bank accounts. You have two, a current account and an investment account. You also have a standing order set up that automatically takes a certain sum out of your current account at the end of each month and pays it into your investment account.

To keep tabs on both you would need to make two separate spreadsheets, each independent of the other. If you link them however then any changes in one will automatically update the other.

Database

Any database is essentially a collection of data stored in such a way as to create easy access to that data when required. Typical examples are mailing lists, customer records and employee details. Until computers came along all this type of data would have been stored using the index card filing system. This method had many inherent problems. It was slow, laborious and prone to mistakes.

Database software is the electronic version of the index card system, with the database itself acting as the filing cabinet, what's known as a *record* being the card, and *fields* that contain the individual bits of information such as names and addresses. Databases that replicate the card system in this way are called flat-file databases.

The real potential of databases is realised in what's known as a relational database management system (RDBMS). This type of set up allows different databases to join forces as it were, to produce extremely powerful cross-referencing. A further bonus is that duplication of data is avoided.

The main advantage of any electronic database is its speed compared to the index card system it's replaced. Using an

Databases and spreadsheets share many functions: for example, they can both be used to store data in table form, and can both sort this data, search through it, etc. The difference between the two is that spreadsheets are designed primarily to analyse numerical data, while databases are designed to store larger amounts of information on an on-going basis for future analysis, reports, mailings, etc.

action known as a *query* or *find*, you type a brief description of what you're looking for into a box provided and then the database dashes off to find it. Within a second or two you're presented with all the information held by the database on the requested subject. It's also easy to amend, add or delete existing data. Bring the information to screen, delete or add data and then re-enter it.

Good programs will provide an indexing facility so that accessing records within a large database is very fast. This is similar to searching the index of a book to help find the required information quickly.

You will find that database programs come with a variety of functions and tools. You will be able to customise your own toolbars and arrange things to suit your own way of working. Like spreadsheets, databases can seem very daunting at first but once you understand the basic principles of how they work, things will quickly become clearer.

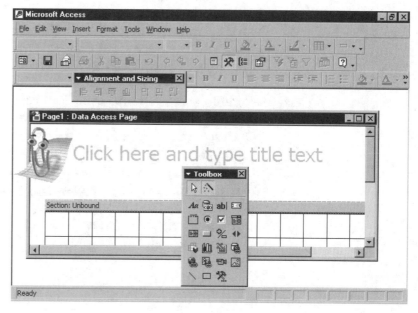

Personal Organiser

A few years ago Filofaxes were all the rage and were designed to help their owners organise their lives, not just socially but at work as well. They included pages for such exciting things as names, addresses, telephone numbers, planners, calendars and useful information such as conversion tables and the like. Nothing that couldn't be kept in a simple diary but for some reason people loved them.

 PDA or hand held computers also have built-in personal organisers to attract people on the move.

They would probably have died a natural death anyway but the arrival of the electronic Filofax, or personal organiser as it is known, finished them off once and for all. These programs come in two versions, one is a little electronic device that can be carried around and the other is a piece of specialised software found on PCs. While they have essentially the same functions as the old paper versions, they do have some major advantages, the PC version in particular.

One such advantage is the wide range of options available when you come to view your data. For example you can set your calendar to display a single page, a week, a month or a year. You can also store almost limitless amounts of information in the electronic version that just wouldn't have been possible with the dog-eared Filofax. When you come to access the information it is presented instantly and clearly as opposed to leafing through tiny pages covered in spidery handwriting. The various functions of the organiser can also be set to integrate with each other so that information entered in, say, the diary, will appear on a particular day in the calendar. The better organisers will provide access to the Internet and e-mail, and Microsoft's Outlook integrates with other office programs too.

Office Suite

The above four programs, the word processor, spreadsheet, database and organiser, taken together as a whole, cover such a wide range of office related applications, that not surprisingly, they are now often lumped together and called Office Suites.

Most PCs today are supplied with an Office Suite such as Microsoft Office, Lotus Smartsuite or Corel Office.

Virtually all PCs sold now come with one of these suites and while it couldn't be said that they are free (the cost will be built in), they will be considerably cheaper than if you were to go out and buy one yourself.

Another advantage is that as all the programs are built by the same manufacturer, they will be designed to integrate with each other in a way that would be impossible to achieve with different programs from different manufacturers.

The main players in this field are Microsoft Office, Lotus Smartsuite and Corel Office. There is little to choose really between the three as they all provide largely the same functions although as with most other things, Microsoft seem to have the edge, particularly when it comes to market share.

Accounts/Finance

Yuk! It's a horrible subject, but to a tremendous amount of people, a very important one. The market for this type of software stems mainly from the business world and this is where the more powerful applications will be found.

Increasingly though, many private individuals and households, are beginning to cotton on to how useful a personal finance package such as Quicken or Microsoft Money can be within a home environment. Budgets can be drawn up and checked they are being kept to, businesses operating from home can be put on a proper financial footing and things like loans, mortgages and investments can all be managed more efficiently. Newer applications will allow you to bank *online* via the Internet, which can be an extremely useful aid for some people who use their bank accounts frequently. While connected up you can visit one of the new share dealing web sites and use your finance program to make you some money.

Professional accounting packages such as Sage Line 50 are very different and are aimed at the business user. Apart from basic Sales, Purchase and Nominal ledgers they provide Invoicing, Banking and various business accounting reports, e.g. VAT return, Profit and Loss, Balance Sheet. However for the average home PC user they will hold little interest, as he or she is never likely to need the facilities these programs provide. Should you ever need to extend one of these systems, perhaps in the case of an expanding business, it's often possible to obtain additional modules, at extra cost. Potential reasons here might be stock control and payroll facilities.

If you purchase a payroll system you should make sure that you will receive updates whenever the Government changes PAYE and NIC regulations.

As a final note it's quite possible for a proficient user to create a tailor made accounts system by using a database or a spreadsheet. This would be quite an undertaking though in terms of both time and effort given the relatively low cost of a good finance program.

Utilities

Given their amazing complexity, the sometimes impossible demands made of them and the hundred and one different things they are often called on to do, PCs, not surprisingly, sometimes get a bit miffed and refuse to play the game. The things they get up to when in this mood can range from the mildly frustrating to the seriously inconvenient.

Fortunately there is an easy way to pacify them and this comes in the form of *Utility* programs. This type of software is designed and written to diagnose and cure the little niggles that irritate PCs and thus make the user's life a bit easier.

 You'll find some functions will be performed by Windows, so you may never need to buy a Utility software package.

Utilities, typically, come with a range of diagnostic and repair tools that will sniff out your PC's ailments and with a bit of luck, put them right. As an example, let's take a program called *Norton Utilities*, which is typical of this genre. This excellent program starts you off with a graphical interface called Utilities Integrator, which is the launching pad for all its tools. These can be classified into four groups – diagnostic/repair, troubleshooting, preventative maintenance and performance enhancement.

In the first group you will find tools such as *system check,* which with one click will examine your entire PC for problems and repair any it finds.

Disk doctor performs a series of surface analysis checks on your drive's disks and automatically carries out repairs if necessary.

Connection Doctor will assist in any connection problems you might have, such as connecting to the Internet. It will also check all your communication ports and modem.

Unerase Wizard is a particularly useful facility that can help you to recover files that have been lost or deleted.

Troubleshooting tools include:

Registry Editor that allows you to get behind the Windows interface and edit the Windows registry that contains all your system's settings. Messing with the Registry can be a hazardous operation so Norton includes an *Undo* feature.

System Information is another very useful facility and it does just what its name suggests. With this tool you can get information on just about anything in your system.

Preventative Maintenance tools include:

System Doctor who sits quietly in the background monitoring what's going on in your PC and will give you advance warning of impending problems such as your hard drive running low on space.

Wipeinfo will remove any trace of selected files from your drives.

Protection adds extra data recovery options to the recycle bin.

Performance Enhancement tools include:

Speed disk which is a defragmentation utility that works considerably faster than the defrag tool supplied by Windows.

Space Wizard provides a safe means of identifying, moving, compressing or deleting files in order to free up disk space.

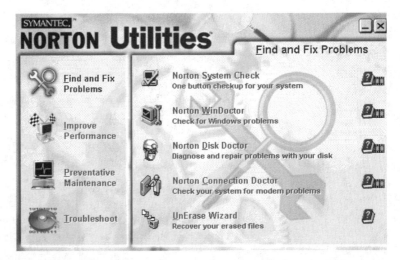

From all this it can be seen that this utility and others of its ilk provide very useful applications which can be used to keep your PC performing at its best. It must be remembered though that they are not fool proof and indeed some of the lower quality utilities not only miss many problems but often *cause* problems, system lock-ups being a typical example. They can also, particularly on slower PCs, be a serious drain on the system's resources, slowing the computer down even further.

Graphics

This is a term given to describe the creation and manipulation of pictures and drawings using computers. The images or drawings may be imported into the program, either by scanning or by cutting or copying them from another application. They can also be created in the graphics program itself. Many word processors, spreadsheets and databases will offer a graphics capability, although these will usually be somewhat basic. Once you have the image where you want it, you can edit it to your heart's content and when happy with the finished article you can decorate your desktop with it, post it to the Web or use it in documents.

A very popular graphics program is Paint Shop Pro. This software is much more powerful than Paint supplied with Windows.

These programs offer a multitude of image editing facilities such as cropping, colour, brightness and contrast controls. They also supply a wide range of special effects which can be further increased in the form of *plug-ins*. Images can be stretched, resized, inverted, zoomed or converted to black and white. Before you start doctoring your favourite holiday snaps though, it's always a good idea to make a copy of the image and use that to experiment on. If you then find you've made a mess of it, you will still have the original.

Many of the facilities will have somewhat obscure names. *Cropping* for example, means cutting off unwanted areas of an image. *Retouch* allows you to determine the strength of the effects you apply. For example you can brush on lightness at a fixed percentage of opacity so that you can build up the effect gradually until you are happy with it.

Cloning is a useful tool with which you can overwrite a specific area with different parts of an image. For example if the picture was a family snapshot ruined by some idiot grinning inanely in the background, you simply brush him out of existence. This feature can also be used to move an object from one image to another. Other tools include filters such as *Despeckle* that removes noise and *Soften* that can be used to remove moire effects.

Once you have your image right you then need to save it and this brings us to graphics file formats. There are two basic types, lossy and lossless. Lossless preserves the file's data in its entirety but for this reason will result in a large file size. Well known lossless formats include BMP, GIF and TIF. Lossy graphics retain much less of the original resulting in much smaller file sizes. A typical lossy format is called JPEG. These various formats are each designed for different applications; GIF is used on Web sites, TIF in publishing and JPEG for general distribution. Good graphics programs will allow you to convert images from one format to another. Another useful facility usually supplied is that of cataloging. You can arrange all your images into albums and view them by means of thumbnails, (small reproductions of the main picture).

...cont'd

Another form of computer graphics is that of Computer Aided Design (CAD). Programs written for this application allow the user to create very complex and technical drawings by use of specialised tools such as 3D rendering. This type of program will mainly be found in business environments where typically they will be used for designing cars and buildings. Professional CAD programs are extremely expensive. For more general PC use though, there are many simple CAD programs about that are still capable of producing excellent drawings.

Microsoft's Powerpoint is a poular present-ation graphics program.

Usually found in the Office suite supplied with your PC will be what's known as a *Presentations* program. These packages specialise in producing graphics on overhead projector foils or on 35mm photographic slides. You can even turn your PC into a slide projector – each picture will be displayed in turn on your screen after a key-press or a short time delay. You can even prepare a slide show specifically to put on the Web.

Desktop Publishing

Desktop Publishing (DTP) is a way of integrating text and graphics on the same page. For the PC owner they are ideal for creating simple documents such as leaflets, newsletters, letterheads and business cards, although with a little effort much more can be accomplished with them. More professional packages such as those used in publishing houses like QuarkXPress and Adobe InDesign, have rendered the traditional method of typesetting virtually obsolete and in so doing have revolutionised the printing industry.

It must be said though, before you rush out and buy one of these programs, that top end word processors such as Microsoft Word, offer many of the same facilities.

You may also decide to invest in a scanner and a laser printer to use with your DTP software.

Multimedia

Multimedia is a name given to describe the concept of integrating various types of media in order to provide an environment conducive to activities such as education, entertainment and relaxation. The media we are talking about here includes sound, video, graphics and text.

The basic concept is nothing new but until fairly recently, the necessary computer technology wasn't available in terms of the system requirements – drive space, RAM, monitor resolution etc, needed for a PC to deal effectively with the combination of tasks required of it. Today, thanks to the cheap and efficient CD-ROM drives and the further development of DVD all that has changed. RAM is now very inexpensive while hard drive capacities have grown out of all recognition. These developments have all been crucial, as video and sound clips demand plenty of storage space.

Education

PCs are marvellous devices for acquiring and displaying all types of information, an ability that is ideally suited to the field of education. More over they can present information in ways much more likely to grab and hold the short attention spans of children for example. How much more

interesting a subject such as Geology will be to them if they can watch video clips of volcanic eruptions accompanied by a sound commentary. Educational software these days range from children's dictionaries and encyclopedias to full GCSE syllabuses.

Reference

Due to the vast storage offered by CDs, complete reference works are now available for the PC owner. Thanks to multimedia you can now not only read about, say, the mysteries of the internal combustion engine you can also watch a computerised animation of the engine actually working.

The breadth and scope of reference material that can be accessed with a computer is breathtaking. Full sets of Encyclopedias, Dictionaries, Atlases, magazines and books are available to anyone who has time to read them.

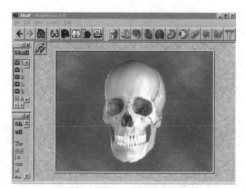

Whole libraries, which in book form would have taken up an entire wall, can now be shovelled into a single drawer.

When it comes to accessing this vast amount of information, the software again shows its class. Modern electronic encyclopedias such as Britannica and Encarta provide search tools that can be as specific or broad as you like. If for example you are writing an essay on the English Civil

War, you can ask the encyclopedia to give you everything it has on the subject. Within seconds you will be presented with a list of dozens, if not hundreds of pertinent articles. Thoughtfully the list is graded with the most likely articles placed at the front of the queue. It must be said that some of the articles will only contain fleeting references to the requested subject but you will at least have them all to hand. Compare this with the daunting task of having to physically wade through probably 20 or 30 full size encyclopedias. If you are looking for something specific then you can use *filters* that will sift out the more unlikely articles, leaving you with a concise list to peruse.

The other tremendous advantage of books in electronic form is that of economics. The complete set of Encyclopedia Britannica can be purchased on CD for around £100, a fraction of what you would pay for it in book form. Moreover all this comes on just two CDs, one if it's a DVD. Also if you have access to the Internet you can update the Encyclopedia regularly at little expense.

Other applications include interactive Atlases, such as Microsoft's Encarta World Atlas, that offer detailed maps of every region of the earth and give a range of map styles such as political, statistical, temperature and climate. There are also detailed histories of each country.

Games

For all the PC's amazing workhorse capabilities, probably its most popular application within the home environment, is that of entertainment, namely game playing. This application has moved on considerably with the advent of Windows. Prior to this getting games set up, never mind playing them, was no mean achievement, involving much fiddling about.

Nowadays you should have little problem running games unless you are using a low specified machine. You really need at least a Pentium 200Mhz or equivalent combined with a good 3Dfx graphics card. Even this will not get the best out of many games with play being slow, jerky, and ultimately, frustrating. The graphics card is the most important element and will take any game into a different dimension.

It's an unfortunate fact that many of the speakers supplied by the manufacturers leave a lot to be desired, although they will be perfectly adequate for general multimedia. To get the best out of your games you really should invest in a decent set. Decent speakers are relatively inexpensive and are well worth the investment. How much more satisfying it would be to blast your opponent out of existence with an ear splitting explosion rather than a pathetic little pop.

While on the subject of sound, it's equally important to have a decent sound card and here you won't go far wrong with a Soundblaster from Creative Labs. A card such as the AWE 32 will give excellent reproduction at a low price.

Another component vital in any games set-up is the controller and like most other PC peripherals, there is a wide range available. These desirable items are by no means essential as any game can be played using the keyboard and mouse, with various keys assigned to different game commands. However this method is only really suitable for the more simple games that have a limited range of commands. For many of the most popular games you simply must have a decent Joystick or Joypad controller. These will open up new options to you and enable you to play your game far more intuitively.

One of the best currently available is the Microsoft Sidewinder Force Feedback Pro. This amazing device not only allows you to play the game in the normal way but also actually physically responds to what's happening in the game. For example fire a gun and you will feel the recoil or rev your Formula One engine and feel the throb of 900 horsepower.

Other good controllers include Microsoft's Sidewinder joypad, which is ergonomically designed with several programmable buttons. For the real drive nut, there are actual mini cockpits complete with steering wheel, gearstick and foot pedals. Not surprisingly these are on the pricey side.

No article on PC gaming would be complete without a mention of the Internet and the whole new dimension it opens up for the gamer. Log on and you will find specialised Web sites such as Microsoft's Gaming Zone. These arenas allow you to compete in your favourite games against real life opponents, although you really do need to watch the phone bill. The Internet also allows you to visit the games manufacturers' sites and download all the latest updates and patches.

 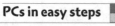

The variety of game types available is considerable. For example there are complex driving games such as Formula One Racing, Touring Car Championship and MotoCross Madness and flight simulators such as European Air War. There are also role playing games like Age of Empires, shoot-em up's, a popular one being Incoming and board games like Chess and Monopoly.

The games industry has grown enormously in recent years and is now worth millions to the manufacturers. This has resulted in tremendous amounts of investment and research with inevitable technological spin-offs that have benefited all PC owners. The levels of realism now offered by the latest games is little short of breathtaking and it will be fascinating to see how far the manufacturers can take it.

Anti-Virus

Before we examine what anti-virus software is we must first understand a particularly unpleasant by-product of the electronic revolution known as a virus. This is a small piece of software written and distributed with the express aim of causing disruption to other people's computer systems. The way these viruses spread is very similar to the way micro-organisms invade our bodies and are then passed on to anybody else who comes into contact with us.

Computer viruses act in just the same way. Any medium that can be inserted into a computer, such as a floppy disk or CD-ROM, can infect a PC with a virus. Viruses passed via floppies are known as *boot sector viruses,* and once in the system remain in the computer's memory infecting any other floppies placed in the PC.

The burgeoning use of the Internet and e-mail has brought with it an ideal medium for the transmission of this type of software. There are millions of web sites in existence today and there are relatively few of them that do not contain downloadable material. This is Utopia to the virus writer,

who having created his virus, can then for example, e-mail it to literally thousands of other PCs. Viruses sent in this way usually attach themselves to executable files or programs. When the program is run, the virus is released and depending on what type it is, can have various nasty effects on your PC.

There are in fact literally thousands of viruses out there, most of which will at worst cause a few minor headaches. For example you might get silly and irritating messages flashing across your screen. On the other hand there are a few which can have devastating consequences to any PC unfortunate enough to contract them. These can cause computers to crash and even wipe all the data off hard drives.

The most common viruses around today thrive within Windows. Usually they are what's called a *Macro* virus and are written using the Visual Basic programming language. When somebody uses Microsoft Word to record a macro, they are using the same language and for this reason Microsoft Word is probably the virus writer's favourite tool. A typical example is that of a virus called Melissa, which was doing the rounds in 1999. Melissa was a macro virus that was stored within a Microsoft Word document. Targets would receive an e-mail to which was attached the said document and when they opened it, out popped Melissa. This evil creature immediately made a beeline for the address book and then e-mailed copies of the document to the first 50 addresses found, thus further propagating herself.

Not all viruses are intended to send data to a computer. There are those that are written with the express intention of *extracting* information from a computer. This point brings us to the question of motivation and just why people write these programs.

In the case of viruses designed to raid computer systems the possible reasons aren't too difficult to understand. Certain types of information will be extremely valuable to the right person who might be persuaded to part with hard cash either to acquire it or to get it back. Revenge and jealousy are other probable motives. Perhaps someone feels they have been unjustly fired by the company they worked for and so decides to get back at the firm by wrecking their databanks.

Computer viruses, particularly the more devious ones, are extremely complex and it takes a clever person to write them. They probably get a perverse sense of 'job satisfaction' out of creating something that can have a devastating impact worldwide.

Anti-virus software is written with the specific aim of detecting these malicious programs and curing the computer of its effects. Just as there are many types of virus, there are many different kinds of anti-virus software, some operating just as deviously as the viruses themselves.

Generic programs for example start by building a database of information on every component of a computer likely to be affected by a virus. If and when the said virus strikes, the program will be able to undo any damage caused by rebuilding the affected files. As an example of how cunning they can be, they can actually 'bait' the computer by creating a file and then keeping a close watch on it to see if anything tries to access it.

Specific anti-virus software are in effect databases which contain details of every known virus, or to put it another way, their *fingerprints.* As soon as a virus invades a PC the program spots it and alerts the user. The main problem with this method is that as soon as a new virus is written, the Specific type of program becomes out of date and so has to be continually updated usually by downloading from the program manufacturer's web site.

Do you need anti-virus software and if so which type should you go for? If you never download from the Net, the chances are you will never contract a virus and thus you are probably quite safe without an anti-virus program. The

Specific programs are generally reckoned to be the best as long as you realise that to keep them working effectively, you must update them on a very regular basis. This necessitates an Internet connection and over a period of time, they will prove to be expensive as the updates aren't handed out for free.

Generic anti-virus software is cheaper in that once you've made the initial purchase, that's it. In theory they are supposed to be able to spot literally any kind of virus but in actual practice they do nothing of the kind. Even if they could how long would it be before some virus writer saw this as a challenge and produced something that was too clever for it?

Voice Recognition

No chapter on software could be complete without mention of what is potentially one of the most significant developments of recent years.

Voice recognition is nothing new, the concept has been around for sometime now and indeed various voice recognition programs have been doing the rounds in the last two or three years. They have never taken off though which is surprising, given what they should be capable of, and indeed are advertised as being capable of.

The problem has been, regardless of the manufacturer's claims, that essentially they haven't been very good, being very difficult to set up, prone to mistakes and susceptible to background interference. Even the latest programs, while improving on earlier efforts, still leave the user having to revert back to his keyboard all too often. The net result has been that while it is possible to create documents by voice recognition, it is still no quicker than using a keyboard and can be considerably more frustrating.

The main reason for this has not been lack of technical ingenuity but more a lack of processing power – voice recognition makes tremendous demands on a computer's resources. It's only now as processing speeds approach the 1000Mhz barrier that the concept is beginning to approach reality.

Voice recognition is a complicated business and initially involves the user 'educating' the software. Typically this involves the user dictating text to the software for a certain period of time, usually between 30 and 60 minutes. This allows the program to create a database of *vocal references*, i.e. the way the user pronounces phonemes (these are the smallest sound units, such as pah or dah). Once the program is set up the user starts dictating into a microphone the text he wants the software to transcribe. Every few milliseconds the analog signal from the microphone is sampled by an analog to digital converter that converts the sound to digital signals. Other factors taken into account at this stage are pitch, volume, frequency and silences. Built into the program is a database, known as a speech engine, which makes further adjustments taking into account such things as background noise, the acoustics of the microphone and from its database of vocal references, the pronunciation peculiarities of the speaker.

Yet another database is comprised of phoneme *models*, averages compiled by sampling the speech of thousands of people. Each factor of the user's speech, such as pitch, is compared against this database to find the entry that most closely matches it. Eventually the software will come up with a phoneme which it thinks most closely resembles the spoken phoneme.

Now these phonemes have to be turned into words. This involves the use of another database, this time of known words. Some words of course, sound the same, but have different meanings, such as pore and poor. These *homonyms*, as they're called, are examined by a database of

grammatical rules that makes an educated guess as to which is the correct word, by examining them in terms of context.

When the program is stumped, it will ask the user to select the correct word from a list it throws up. It makes a note of the choice made and enters the details into its databases for future reference and in this way the software learns from its mistakes.

Once firmly established and supported with the necessary hardware, voice recognition systems are going to revolutionise our lives. The list of possibilities for this technology is literally endless, ranging from the mundane such as telling your television to switch itself on to channel 3, to opening up a new world for people with serious physical disabilities.

Peripherals

Given a computer in its basic form, you'll be very limited in what you can achieve with it. Rather like a game of football without goal posts. Sure, you'll be able to kick the ball about but it'll all be pointless because you will never be able to score a goal. To be able to achieve a particular goal with a computer you need devices that will let you enter and remove data. These devices are called peripherals and this chapter introduces you to the main types.

Covers

Chapter Five

Introduction

Peripherals is a term used to describe components that aren't inherent in a basic computer system and are not considered essential to the operation of such a system. An analogy here could be the train set you had as a child (or wished you'd had). Initially you would have started off with an engine, a few pieces of track and a couple of carriages. This would have been enough to get you started but it wouldn't have been long before you started adding to the basic set, i.e. more engines, scenery, a signal box, etc., to increase its capacity and entertainment value.

In the same way a PC system will initially be comprised of just the basic components needed to make it work, monitor, keyboard, mouse, basic software, etc. After you've explored the possibilities of the initial set-up and made some decisions as to what you are going to use the PC for, the need for extra items, or peripherals, will manifest itself. Just as in the software market, the range of add-ons for the PC is enormous and can put a serious strain on your wallet. Again, as with software, there are many manufacturers competing against each other for your custom, all promising high quality at the lowest possible prices. To the uninitiated the specifications quoted on the advertising blurb can be at best confusing, at worst completely baffling. Most of these manufacturers are reputable and you can buy their products with the knowledge that they will generally do what they say it will (most of it anyway). There are exceptions however to every rule and this applies equally here.

The intention of this section is to familiarise you with the types of peripheral on offer, the pros and cons and to explain what they do and how they do it. Along the way, some of the technology and jargon the manufacturers use, should become clearer and this will help you to come to the right decisions.

Printer

A few years ago it was widely believed that the computer revolution would very rapidly lead to the so-called 'paperless office'. Certainly the trees were interested in the concept but sadly it just didn't materialise. Twenty years on and the rainforests are still shrinking as our electronic gadgets swallow up more paper than ever before. There are several reasons for this, the main one being, without doubt, our inherent distrust of computers. This really isn't surprising given the propensity of the things to crash, so what do we do? We make hard copies of our work, just to be on the safe side. So as far as the trees are concerned, nothing has changed. Another reason is the low prices at which quality printers are now being sold and the speed at which they can work. Everybody can afford one and so they *have* one. *Having* a thing means you must *use* it.

Consider also the capabilities of modern day printers. Gone are the days when they could only produce black text with maybe a handful of different font types in simple and standard formats. Today's machines are just as comfortable with colour as they are with text. Not only can text be printed out in any colour under the sun but also in any one of literally thousands of different font sizes and types. They can also, most importantly, print pictures and with photographic quality at that. This has opened up whole new applications for these devices – personalised stationery, business cards, flyers, newsletters, greetings cards and company reports complete with coloured graphs and charts, to name just a few.

And so we are back to paper. To utilise the wonderful capabilities offered by this new breed of printer, we need paper, endless and continuously increasing amounts of the stuff. It's actually become more important than ever. The humble machine of yesteryear, noisily clacking away while churning out realms of ugly black text has now developed into the most essential of computer peripherals.

There are many different types of printer all with their own specialist applications, but essentially they all do the same thing, produce hard copy. The ways that they achieve this vary and we will now look at some of these machines and their principles of operation.

Dot Matrix

The noisy, uninspiring printer referred to above would have in all likelihood been a dot matrix printer. Essentially there was nothing wrong with them, they got the job done, although painfully slowly by today's standards.

These printers work by using a printing head that literally fires pins at the paper. Between the head and the paper is an ink saturated ribbon, and as the pins strike the ribbon, they transfer the ink onto the paper. The characters created are comprised of a pattern of dots, the more dots, the better the print quality. Dot matrix printers are supplied with print heads containing either 9 or 24 pins and the 24 pin versions can produce surprisingly good results. Some of these printers improve the output quality by making a second pass across the paper and printing out another series of dots slightly offset from the first. The disadvantage here is that it halves the print speed which can vary from some 180 characters per second (CPS) to over 360 CPS.

Dot matrix printers are ideal for printing on multi-part, continuous invoice stationery.

Dot matrix printers are ideal for printing out on long rolls of continuous stationary, a facility that makes them invaluable for use in shop environments for example. The electronic till which gives you your receipt will be printed by this method.

Ink Jet

Ink jet printers are similar in operation to dot matrix in that the printhead makes passes across the paper, the difference here is that instead of physically forcing the ink onto the paper, it fires the ink directly onto the paper. This does away with the need for ribbons. However, the ink must come from somewhere and so they are supplied with ink cartridges, usually two in the better quality printers. One cartridge will contain only black ink and the other will have three colours, cyan, yellow and magenta. These cartridges are comprised of ink filled firing chambers, each of which are connected to a minute nozzle (thinner than a human hair). When requested to print, the machine first heats the ink to boiling point, this process causing it to bubble. As the bubble expands it forces the ink through the nozzles onto the paper. The ink then cools, causing the bubble to collapse, resulting in a sucking action that pulls fresh ink from the chamber.

The amount of ink dots the printer produces determines the print quality and these days range from 300 dots per inch (dpi) up to 1400 dpi. Printers giving an output of 600 dpi will produce letter quality and be more than adequate for general home use. If you want top notch performance though you need to look at 1400 dpi, particularly if you want photographic quality printing.

The plus points of ink jets are firstly their price. Given the quality of their output, they really are amazingly cheap these days, a good quality 600 dpi model can now be had for about £100. As already stated the quality they produce is excellent while another point to consider is the software supplied with these machines.

This provides the user with all sorts of useful options. You can set the print quality, number of copies required, print in reverse order and adjust the colour settings. Also supplied will be maintenance tools that will allow you to clean the print nozzles and adjust printhead alignment.

Unfortunately it's not all sweetness and light. Ink jets do have their negative aspects, one of which is their running costs. While the ink cartridge method they employ produces excellent prints, the cartridges themselves don't hold a great amount of ink. This is not so much of a problem when using black text, or even coloured text for that matter. However try printing out a batch of colour leaflets for example and you will soon be reaching for your wallet again. What's more the cartridges are not cheap – what the manufacturers are losing by supplying the machine itself cheaply, they are clawing back via the

One way to save money with ink cartridges is to refill them yourself. Special kits are available for this purpose and can be found in the advertising sections of computer magazines.

consumables. Also while the printer software will often give you a bar indicator showing the level of ink remaining in the cartridges, it's still very difficult to know exactly what the anticipated print life of these cartridges is. The manufacturers of course make claims on this point but these are usually wildly optimistic, being based on ideal operating conditions. Having said all this, if your printing requirements are limited to the occasional letter or photo, then you should be Ok for a few months.

The other factor to take into account is the paper itself. For black text virtually any type of paper will do but if you are planning to print photographs, you will need specially coated glossy paper that prevents the different colours bleeding into each other. This does not come cheaply and you can expect to pay up to 25p per sheet.

To sum up, ink jet printers will provide excellent print quality, quickly and at very reasonable prices. They can however be very expensive to run, the cost obviously being proportional to the amount of use they're given. For general purpose use though, they are ideal.

Laser
For high volume requirements, such as in the busy office, laser printers will be the best option. In the same way that ink jets are a considerable improvement on the dot matrix, the laser is yet another step up for basically the same reasons. The quality they offer is higher than the ink jet (approaching typeset quality), and the speed at which they operate is also much greater. Not surprisingly they are also more expensive.

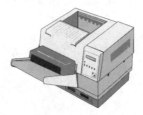

The reason for this is the complexity of the machines. Every time you activate a laser printer you are putting into motion a highly organised and integrated sequence of events controlled by a microprocessor.

The principle of operation is similar to that employed by the photocopier, whereby beams of laser light and a system of optical components are used to etch images on a photoconductor drum from which they are carried via electrostatic photocopying, to paper. The document to be printed, instead of being copied a character at a time, is instead transferred in its entirety. For this reason the printing speed of these printers is quoted in pages per minute. The range of options available with these laser printers is considerable, for example, the ability to print on both sides of the paper, called *duplexing*. Or you might be producing a series of documents in which the covering page is letterheaded and the following pages plain. In this instance you would need a machine with two paper bins.

As with everything else laser printers are not perfect and there are several factors to be considered when evaluating them. Again, we have the issue of the manufacturers' quoted claims for print speeds. These are always the maximum possible and taken when the printer is working under optimal conditions. In practice, the true speed achieved will be influenced by a host of other factors such as the type of document, its graphical content and resolution. The cheaper lasers do not have their own microprocessor, instead relying on the PC to do all the processing. This is known as host based printing and while it does not affect the output quality, it does mean that the general performance of the printer is largely dependent on the PC that is controlling it. Another point here is that the operating system will almost certainly have to be Windows, other systems are rarely supported.

If you are planning to produce documents that are mainly graphic in content, you will need to ensure that the printer's memory is large enough to store the entire image. Remember that these machines print by the page rather than by the character.

Colour laser printers are relatively new on the block and can cost thousands of pounds while monochrome lasers can now often be picked for up for little more than the cost of an equivalent ink jet. They are however beginning to drop in price and it probably won't be that long before mid quality lasers are an affordable option for the PC owner.

Scanner

A scanner essentially uses the same technology as a fax machine. It reads an image from paper and instead of sending it down the telephone line, converts it to a format that your PC can understand. The computer holds the image as a graphics file, which you can print, amend or add to other documents.They are extremely useful devices and come in three main types (sheet-fed, flatbed and hand-held) that differ primarily in the way that the material is scanned.

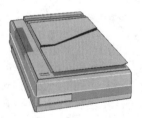

Sheet-fed scanners employ a system of rollers to move the paper past the scan head, whereas in a flatbed scanner the opposite occurs, the scan head is moved over the paper. There are pros and cons with both of these methods. For example in a flatbed scanner, an arrangement of mirrors is needed to keep the scanned image focused on the image sensors. The image will suffer from a certain degree of degradation because of inherent imperfections in the mirrors. The flatbed's big advantage however, is that it can be used to scan large bulky documents such as a book. The sheetfed scanner will reproduce an image more accurately but you can only scan material that falls within the machine's physical capacity, i.e. single sheets of paper.

Hand held scanners are a compromise in that they don't need the mirror focussing system but can still be used to scan the pages of a book. The drawback lies in the fact that they are hand held. Unsteady hands don't make for great scanning results. However they don't need mechanical mechanisms so they are the cheapest of the three types.

 To scan photo-graphic transpar-encies to very high professional quality, go to a bureau utilising a drum scanner – these are very expensive to buy.

To illustrate how these devices work we'll take a look at a flatbed scanner. This basically consists of a plastic lidded box. Open the lid and you will see a glass surface. This is where the document to be scanned is placed, face down. An internal light is passed through red, green and blue filters to illuminate the document, the idea being that the blank spaces between the individual letters will reflect more light than the darker letters will.

A motorized scanning head then moves across the page, capturing as it does so, the light reflected from minute sections of the page. The reflections are then passed through an arrangement of mirrors that focuses the light on to a set of light sensitive diodes. These diodes convert the light into an electrical current, the strength of which is dependent on the amount of light.

A small processor, known as an analog to digital converter, receives the signals and further converts them into binary code. It is then passed to the PC where it is stored in a format that enables the user to access the data via a suitable application such as a graphics program.

These devices are great tools and add further to the range of tasks to which a PC can be put. A typical example is that of your photograph collection. Scanners are ideally suited for scanning all your favourite snapshots and then storing them in easily accessible electronic photo albums within the PC. An advantage of doing this is that the scanned picture will never fade with time as does the paper version.

Scanners are available at amazingly low prices nowadays. Perfectly respectable ones can be picked up for £50 and for the average PC user, will give very pleasing results. When buying your scanner pay attention to the build quality as some of them can have very flimsy lid hinges. Another thing to watch out for, as always, are the manufacturers' claims regarding maximum scan resolutions. Typically these are advertised at up to 9600 dpi and with colour resolutions of 36 bit (which means over 68 billion different colours). What does all this mean? Not a lot is the honest answer. When you consider that the human eye is only capable of discerning some 16 million different colours (24 bit), then really what is the point of 68 billion? Basically they're conning you into spending more money than you need to, so take all these figures with a big pinch of salt.

Modem

One of the prime reasons these days that people buy PCs is to get on to the Internet. The Internet is not just an extension of the PC though, it's an entity in its own right and to gain access you need a connection to it via your telephone. This is where the modem comes in. As we already know, the computer is a digital device whereas the telephone is an analog device. To enable the two different systems to work together, we need a device to convert data between the two formats. This is what the modem does. Digital information from the computer is converted (modulated) to analog and analog data from the telephone system is converted (demodulated) to digital.

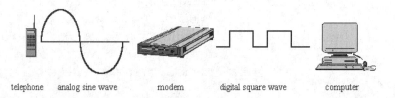

| telephone | analog sine wave | modem | digital square wave | computer |

The two terms *mod*ulate and *dem*odulate combine to give the modem its name. For an Internet connection to be possible there must be a modem at each end of the connection and data transfer will only be as fast as the slower of the two modems allows.

These devices are standard and there's really not much difference between them other than the speed at which they operate. External modems are a separate unit that will connect to your PC via one of its ports, but more commonly these days, modems are being supplied as internal units in the form of an expansion card plugged into the motherboard. A couple of years ago modem transfer rates of 28.8 Kb per second were common, nowadays speeds of 56 Kb are the norm. A feature supplied with any good modem these days is the ability to send and receive faxes.

So what do you look for when buying or upgrading a modem? Firstly it should be 'BT approved', meaning that it isn't going to destroy the local exchange when you switch it on. Then you must decide whether to go for an external or internal modem. Internal modems will cost less because they will draw their power from the PC's power supply, while an external modem will need its own supply. However with the external modem you will have a better idea of what it's doing via its panel lights. They will also need desk space, which is an important consideration when you think of all the other peripherals you are likely to have.

The next issue is that of data transfer speed, measured in Kbs per second. The fastest modem speed at the moment is 56 Kb and given that they don't cost that much more than the slower models, it's worth going for one of these. Bear in mind though that this figure is a theoretical maximum and that in all likelihood it will never achieve anything like that speed. The reasons for this range from the quality of the phone line you are using to the speed of the service provider's modem. Finally your chosen modem should be capable of sending and receiving faxes. If it can't then it probably can't do much else either.

Digital Camera

Digital cameras can be very roughly equated with scanners, in the sense that they will drop an image into a PC, but that really is where the resemblance ends. They only have one possible use, which is to take a photograph and then download it into a computer for possible editing and then storage.

When digital cameras first made their appearance in the market place, they were pitched at the growing army of Internet users who needed some way of getting pictures into their PCs before they could then post them on the Web. The initial response was sluggish to say the least due to the usual reasons of cost and quality. There were not many people willing to pay twice as much for a camera that produced image quality half as good as a film camera. Gradually though as the technology developed, prices dropped while the quality improved.

The situation now is completely different, with almost every major camera manufacturer, jostling to get in on the act. Prices have now dropped to the point where a good digital camera can be had for £200 or £300 whilst at the same time providing quality good enough for most purposes. At the higher end of the market, digital cameras costing between £600 and £900 are now beginning to throw down a serious challenge to their film based cousins. While the general concensus at the moment is that film still reigns supreme, particularly for the professional photographer, it's also felt that it's just a matter of time before digital cameras catch up.

The reason for their increasing popularity, apart from the fact that they are now affordable, is their sheer simplicity and ease of use. Because they are electronic devices they do all the work for you. Simply aim it at something interesting and press the button. No more fiddling about with aperture settings, film speed and the like. Having taken your snaps you can immediately download them on to your PC, where you can then play around with them to your heart's desire.

The advantages are obvious. Firstly you eliminate the cost of buying film and then having it developed. There is no delay factor, i.e. you no longer have to wait until the film is used up before having it developed. Being stored in the PC, your photos will be more accessible and furthermore will never degrade over time. You can print out hard copies or use them to make personalised greeting cards or stationery. Their potential in business applications is equally obvious. Products can be easily and cheaply photographed for inclusion in presentations and the like.

So how do they work? Like all things computer based, the principle lies with converting data from one format to another and then back again to the original. With the digital camera we start with the lens that works in exactly the same way as it does in a film camera. Light passes through the lens, which focuses it on a chip called a charge coupled device (CCD). This chip is covered with transistors that create electrical signals in proportion to the intensity of the light striking them. These signals are in analog form and pass through an *analog to digital converter (ADC)*. This chip converts the analog signals to a digital format and then sends it along to another chip called a *Digital Signal Processor (DSP)* that is designed specifically to deal with photographic images. This chip makes adjustments to the image, such as contrast and brightness, compresses it and then sends it to the camera's storage device. When the user is ready to view his picture he simply downloads it to the PC through a suitable cable. Some cameras use a floppy disk for this purpose, which can be used in the usual manner. More recent developments are in the form of flash cards, which are basically memory chips mounted on a small printed circuit board. These plug into a special port on the PC.

For more inform- ation about digital cameras and photography see Digital Photography in easy steps.

Things to look out for when buying a digital camera include the following: resolution of at least 800x600 if you are looking for quality images. A feature to allow image compression is also useful. The optics should be of good quality and ideally will include an optical zoom. Also an automatic focus feature will give clearer images than fixed focus will. An LCD preview screen will allow you to be more selective about what you photograph and ensure more efficient use of the camera's memory. The more memory it has, the more pictures you can take. Another extremely useful extra is a TV connector and cable. This will allow you to display your snaps on the telly.

Zip Drive

Probably the most popular storage and back up device on the market, the Iomega Zip drive is relatively cheap, easy to install, provides reliable performance and good storage capacities. They can be used externally by simply plugging them into a spare port at the back of your PC or you can mount them internally in a spare drive bay. These drives operate in the same way as the floppy drive but the big difference is in the drive disk itself. Whereas the floppy disk can hold a maximum of 1.44Mb, the Zip disk can hold 100Mb, the equivalent of 70 floppies.

It does this in two ways. Firstly the magnetic material used to coat the disk has a much higher energy level than that used with the floppy disk, which means it is more efficient when it comes to storing data. Secondly, the zip drive uses much smaller read/write heads, allowing it to write over 2000 data tracks per inch in comparison to the 135 tracks per inch written by the floppy drive. The other big advantage of the Zip drive over the floppy, is its rapid data access speed, comparable to low end hard drives.

The Iomega range also includes larger capacity drives including the recently released Zip 250, that uses disks with a capacity of 250 Mb.

 Zip drives are supplied with software that automates back up procedures for you. Simply select your file and specify where you want it backed up to and the software does the rest.

Jaz Drive

The Iomega Jaz is the Zip's big cousin and uses disks with storage capacities of up to 2Gb. Two or three of these disks and you could back up the entire contents of a hard drive. The drawback is that this would be a comparatively expensive way of doing things as 2Gb Jaz disks cost about £70 a piece, equating to £35 per Gb.

Given the high cost of the Jaz system, if you really are looking for this level of storage, it is seriously worth considering adding a second hard drive to your computer. For £140, just twice the cost of a Jaz disk, you could buy a new hard drive of 17 Gb. This works out at just over £8 per Gb. Add to this equation the cost of the Jaz drive itself (about £250) and it begins to make sense. You do however have the problem of installing the hard drive whereas the Jaz is easy to install and comes with the further advantage of being transportable.

Tape Back Up

An alternative and more cost effective means of large scale storage and back up is provided by tape systems, the most traditional and used method of all. These systems work in much the same way as your video recorder does, only on a more advanced level. Indeed, there have been attempts made to use video cassettes as a PC storage medium but the method wasn't really practical and so never caught on. Of more practical use are the specialised drive systems. These use tape cassettes that simply plug in and out of your machine. The capacities of these tapes can be enormous, an asset that makes them ideal for large scale back up in office and business environments. Another big plus is the fact that the media they employ, i.e. tape, is the cheapest one of all.

Remember that while tape systems are very cheap, they cannot be accessed in the same way as other drive systems. You have to physically forward and rewind the tape until you find the required data. This can be a very slow and tedious business.

These tape systems however do come with several disadvantages not the least of which is their serial nature. They are not like a disk drive, which you can open up and from the contents displayed, select the file or folder you want. To write and read data from a tape you have to physically wind and rewind the tape, which can be an extremely tedious task. For unattended complete back up or restoral this doesn't matter so much, but if you are working with specific files, it could turn you grey over night. Also you cannot edit material stored in this way. Another serious shortcoming they have is their magnetic nature, i.e. external sources of magnetism such as speakers or monitors, can destroy the contents of a tape cassette. They are also more prone to heat and physical abuse.

CD-R and CD-RW

On page 25 we described how a CD-ROM drive worked and how its media, i.e. the CD, was capable of holding up to 650 Mb of data. The ordinary CD however is not capable of being written to, it can only be read.

A fairly recent development of the CD drive system is what is known as CD-R (CD recordable) and CD-RW (CD rewritable). Let's first consider the CD-R. It works in basically the same way as the ordinary CD-ROM that uses a laser beam to read data. With the CD-R drive system however, the CD itself is different, it is capable of being written to by the laser, in a method known as write-once, read-many (WORM). This allows the user to create his own CD disks, although once created, he won't be able to make any changes to it. The data is stored permanently.

A further refinement of this system comes in the form of CD-RW drives. As with all types of CD drives, the writing process employs a laser which physically alters the surface characteristics of the CD by literally 'burning' in the data in the form of tiny pits. Once done, the data cannot be altered.

The rewritable drive gets round this by using a different, lower energy, laser beam in a process known as *annealing*. This beam heats the data pits on the CD to a point where they recrystallize to their original state. The CD can then be reused. Thus we now have the happy situation of being able to use a CD in exactly the same way as we would a hard drive.

Things are getting even better though. Digital Video Disks (DVD) as we have already seen, are capable of holding truly monstrous amounts of data for their size – up to 17Gb. The same rewriteable technology is now being applied to them and DVD-RW drives are already on the market. As with any new technology, they are not cheap at the moment. Prices though will inevitably drop as they become more common.

Summary of Storage/Backup Drives

This section analyses the cost per Gigabyte, of the various media considered above and reveals some surprising facts.

Floppy Disks	694 disks needed	cost approx. £200
Zip 100	10 disks needed	cost approx. £100
Zip 250	4 disks needed	cost approx. £60
Jaz 1Gb	1 disk needed	cost approx. £70
Jaz 2Gb	1/2 disk needed	cost approx. £37
Hard Drive	assuming 10Gb disk	cost approx. £10
Tape	assuming 12Gb tape	cost approx. £2
CD-R	2 disks needed	cost approx. £2
CD-RW	2 disks melded	cost approx. £25

This table shows that in terms of storage capability, the floppy disk is actually twice as expensive as any other while at the same time being the least efficient. Hard drives show up well, particularly when you consider that they are the most efficient of the lot. They are however much more difficult to install. Tape and CD-R come out as the cheapest storage media by some way. However as CD-R allows selective access to its contents and is also much faster than tape cassettes, this media appears to be the clear winner at the moment.

Upgrading

Unless a bottomless pit of money is available, to keep any computer system up to date, it will periodically have to be upgraded. Many people see this as the province of the computer engineer and it never occurs to them to have a go themselves. For those of you who are a bit more adventurous, we will run through the procedures necessary for the usual upgrades.

Covers

Chapter Six

Introduction

There will inevitably come a time when you decide that some element of your system can be improved upon. Alternatively a new use for your PC might become apparent which will require the installation of a new component. Computer technology is growing at an ever expanding rate, to the point where systems are becoming obsolete almost as they are rolling down the production line. It's a certain fact that the computer you buy, will within a matter of months, be available for a lower price and will probably include better features to boot. If you are one of those who likes to keep at the cutting edge, then you need to do something about this. Obviously it's out of the question to buy a completely new system every few months, so the only practical solution is to keep upgrading the machine you have.

Before attempting any major upgrade do read the relevant section in your PC's manual. These contain technical data that can be very useful.

Computers lend themselves to this quite readily due to the modular nature of their construction. This feature allows you to replace individual components on a need-to basis while leaving the rest of the system intact. Obviously many people are not going to have the slightest inclination to pull their PC apart so the only option here is to take the computer to a dealer who will do the work for you. Equally obvious is the fact that this will significantly increase the cost of the upgrade while at the same time leaving you without your PC for probably quite a while.

For a more detailed discussion of updating your PC's hardware and software, read Upgrading Your PC in easy steps.

However, many upgrades are surprisingly simple to do, requiring little more than a screwdriver. You will also find that having successfully completed your first upgrade, that you will be much more confident about tackling the next one. In no time at all you will be wondering just what it was that you were so worried about. Another thing to be said for doing your own upgrades is that you will learn a considerable amount about your PC in the process. For these reasons it is strongly recommended that you have a go, you have little to lose and a great deal to gain.

As you use your PC over a period of time, you will begin to appreciate its limitations. Various things will become obvious to you. For example as you load more and more programs onto your hard drive, you might find that it's beginning to struggle to find room for them all. A year or two down the line, your youngest son might develop an interest in the latest computer games, which might necessitate upgrading the graphics card. As you leaf through the computer magazines and read about the latest Intel 650Mhz processor, you might start looking at your old Pentium 200Mhz chip in a rather different light.

When you do make the decision to at least have a look inside the case, there are a few basic rules you must follow. Firstly and most importantly, switch the thing off. It sounds painfully obvious but there are still people who don't. While there are no lethal voltages within the system case, it really doesn't make sense to take chances.

Secondly you must earth yourself to get rid of any electrostatic electricity. The little tingle that does nothing more than give you a slight start, will devastate the chips on your PC's circuit boards.

The next thing is to identify the various components. There aren't very many of them so this shouldn't present any difficulty. There should also be a suitable diagram in the PC's manual that will help. A little common sense doesn't go amiss either. For example you should by now know, that the graphics card is the interface between the PC and the monitor. It follows from this that if you are trying to identify this board, simply follow the cable from the monitor and see where it connects to.

One of the first things you should notice is a large circuit board screwed to one side of the case. This is the motherboard and will contain all the RAM chips and also the CPU. Plugged into the motherboard will be the expansion cards such as your modem or sound card. At the top rear will be a large metal box, which will be the power supply. From this will be various leads and connectors that go to other parts of the system. Finally, at the front of the case you will find the drive bays. Here will be the hard drive, the floppy drive and the CD-ROM drive.

Hard Drive

Installing a new hard drive is probably one of the more interesting experiences you will share with your PC. However as long as you know what to do before you start, it's really not that big a deal. The reasons for doing so are obvious enough; you need more storage capacity.

Absolutely the first thing you must do is find your CD boot disk, the manufacturer should have supplied one with the PC. Remember the hard drive is what the computer boots from, it contains the Windows start up files. Your new drive will not and so for this purpose will be useless. It'll be like trying to start a car with the plugs removed. It just won't happen. This is where the CD boot disk comes in. It'll enable the PC to get as far as the Windows installation program.

The second thing you must do is to identify the correct jumper setting at the rear of the new drive. Refer to the documentation for this. You'll find that there are various options available depending on whether the new drive is to be the main (master) drive or a secondary (slave) drive. In our case the drive is going to be the master.

Now disconnect the old drive from the power supply and motherboard. Be careful to note which way round the connections go. Often they will only go in one way but not always. Remove the drive by undoing the screws on either side and replace it with the new one. Now re-connect the power supply and motherboard cable.

This is where the fun starts. Switch the computer on and as soon as you see a message saying *hit delete to enter set-up*, do so. This will take you into the BIOS settings from where you will be able to 'introduce' your new hard disk drive to the system. You will see various options one of which will read *Ide HDD Auto Detection.* Using the arrow keys navigate your way here and press enter.

You will see a new message asking you to *select primary master.* Under this you will see the details of your new drive. Hit enter. You will now see three more screens in succession asking you to select *secondary master, primary slave* and *secondary slave* respectively. Keep hitting enter until you are back to the original BIOS screen.

Go to *save set-up and exit* and hit enter. You will be asked to confirm by typing the letter Y. Do so and hit enter again. Now go to *Standard CMOS set-up* and press enter. If everything has gone to plan you will see your new drive confirmed as the primary master.

Hit Esc and you will leave the BIOS and the computer will restart. Now we enter the murky netherworld of DOS. At the DOS prompt type FDISK and hit enter. Before your new drive can be used it must be *partitioned*, or 'made useable'. The first thing you will see is a long message that says:

Your computer has a disk larger than 512 MB. This version of Windows includes improved support for larger disks, resulting in more efficient use of disk space on large drives, and allowing disks over 2 GB to be formatted as a single drive. IMPORTANT: if you enable large disk support and create any new drives on this disk, you will not be able to access the new drive(s) using other operating systems, including some versions of Windows 95 and Windows NT, as well as earlier versions of Windows and MS-DOS. In addition, disk utilities will not be able to work with this disk. If you need to access this disk with other operating systems or older disk utilities, do not enable large drive support.

*Do you wish to enable large drive support <Y/
N>...............?(Y)*

Ignore this message and hit enter. You will now see a DOS
window giving you 4 options. Select option 1 which says
Create DOS Partition or Logical DOS Drive. Hit enter. In
the new window that appears select option 1, which will say
Create Primary DOS Partition. Hit enter.

You will now be given the option of how big to make your
partition. For example if you choose 100%, the partition
will be 100% of the new drive. If you choose 50%, then
your new drive will be split up into two equal sections, and
each will be treated by the system as a completely separate
drive, with half the real drive capacity. For example, when
you go into *My Computer*, instead of just seeing a hard
drive icon for Drive C, you will also see one for Drive D. If
the capacity of the drive you are installing is 10Gb, then
each of the two new drives will have capacities of 5Gb.

Assuming you choose a partition size of 100%, hit enter
and you will be told that a *Primary DOS Partition Has Been
Created.* This part of the procedure is now finished. Exit
FDISK by hitting the *Esc* key and you will be presented
with the DOS prompt again.

Now the new drive must be formatted, i.e. a folder and file
structure must be created to enable Windows to use the
drive. At the prompt type FORMAT C: here 'C' is the drive
to be formatted. After a warning message advising you that
formatting will destroy all data on the drive, the formatting
procedure will take place. How long this takes depends on
the size of the drive and the speed of your computer, but it
shouldn't take longer than half an hour.

When finished exit DOS. Now insert your CD boot disk in
the floppy drive and your Windows CD in the CD-ROM
drive and restart the PC. From here on in it will be a simple
matter of following the on-screen commands. It sounds
more complicated than it is. A good idea is to have a trial
run beforehand: go into the BIOS and FDISK programs to
see if there is anything that might faze you.

Central Processing Unit

Considering its pivotal role in the computer, upgrading a CPU is not the complex operation you might expect it to be. It is in fact one of the easier upgrades you can make as long as a few conditions are met.

Before you do so however, be quite certain that it actually needs upgrading. Many people, when their PC starts slowing down, automatically assume that a new CPU is the order of the day. This isn't always the case though. The main cause of the problem might well be insufficient RAM to cope with the extra workload being placed on it by all the increasingly resource hungry applications you are running. How do you know though?

One easy way is to run a system utility program such as Norton Utilities, described on pages 125–126. This program will tell you anything you want to know about your system including how much RAM you have available at any one time.

Let's assume however that a new CPU is what you want, for whatever the reason. The actual process with today's computers is very simple. The CPU will be plugged into the motherboard. All you need to do is unplug it and replace it with the new one. Before you go out and buy one though you must ensure that it will be compatible with the motherboard. The easiest way to do this is to give the manufacturer of your PC a ring and speak to their technical department. Tell them what you are proposing to do and they will be able to advise you accordingly.

RAM

 When upgrading RAM, it's all too easy to buy the wrong type. To avoid this contact the manufacturer's technical department first and they will be able to tell you exactly what you need.

Upgrading your system's memory can have a startling effect on your PC's overall performance and as with the CPU, is an extremely simple upgrade to carry out. There are quite a few different types of RAM chip about and it's essential that you buy the right type for your system. Here's a brief description of the more common types.

Static Random Access Memory (SRAM)

A single memory chip is made up of several million memory cells. In a SRAM chip, each memory cell consists of a single flip-flop (for storing the binary digits 1 or 0) and a few more transistors (for reading or writing operations).

Dynamic Random Access Memory (DRAM)

In a DRAM chip, each memory cell consists of a capacitor (rather than a flip-flop) and a single transistor. When a capacitor is electrically charged, it is said to store the binary digit 1, and when discharged, it represents 0; these changes are controlled by the transistor. Since it has fewer components, DRAM requires a smaller area on a chip than does SRAM, so a DRAM chip can have a greater memory capacity, though its access time is slower than SRAM.

Extended Data Out Random Access Memory (EDO RAM)

This type of chip can send data even while decoding instructions about its next move. Very fast and often found in Pentium PCs.

Synchronous Dynamic Random Access Memory (SDRAM)

This chip is an advanced version of the DRAM chip and has been designed to keep pace with the faster bus speeds of the latest CPUs. They come with two banks of transistors for increased performance.

These are the main types applicable to today's PCs. There is however a further consideration with these chips and this concerns the way they are presented to the motherboard. The term used here is *module* and whichever type of chip your PC uses, they will come in the form of either *Single In Line Memory Modules (SIMM)* or *Double In Line Memory Modules (DIMM)*. These modules are basically little circuit boards on which are mounted the chips. Along one edge of the board will be a row of connectors that enable it to be plugged into a special socket on the motherboard. The boards are asymmetrical so that it's impossible to install them the wrong way round. The difference between SIMMs and DIMMs is simply that the DIMM module has chips mounted on both sides of the board, doubling its capacity. 64Mb of RAM in a DIMM module will take up no more space than 32Mb of RAM in a SIMM module.

A potential headache when adding extra RAM is the physical capacity offered by the motherboard. A good board will have two sockets, which provides ample room for expansion. Some motherboards will only have one though so when you come to add extra memory, you will find there's nowhere to install it. Then the only thing you can do is remove the old RAM chips and replace them with a higher capacity module.

To determine exactly what you need, as with a CPU upgrade, the easiest way is to contact the manufacturer. When actually handling the chip do make sure that you have earthed yourself. Take care when installing the RAM module, the connecting pins are very fragile and won't appreciate being forced into position.

CD-ROM and Floppy Drives

Installing these devices is easy: open up the system case, locate the device to be replaced and disconnect the cables. Undo the screws and remove it. Put the new drive in its place and secure it with the screws. Reconnect the cables and replace the case's cover. These devices will come with a driver, usually supplied on a floppy disk.

Place the driver floppy into the floppy disk drive and then fire up the PC. The driver should automatically install. If it doesn't, go into *My Computer* and click the floppy drives icon. This will reveal the contents of the floppy disk and all you do is locate the *set-up* or *install* file and click it.

Expansion Cards

Expansion cards are printed circuit boards that plug into the computer's motherboard via its expansion slots. There are three types, ISA, PCI and AGP.

Most expansion cards today will be designed to be compatible with your PCI slots. An exception to this could be a graphics card many now plug into the AGP slot – a port designed for these cards.

The advantage of expansion cards is that they enable the user to integrate hardware with their system, thus freeing up space on a cluttered desk.

Applications that come in the form of expansion cards include graphics cards, modems, sound cards, SCSI adapters, and TV tuner cards.

The installation of these cards is simple and to illustrate how it's done we will consider a graphics card upgrade. First you need to make room for the card by unscrewing a metal strip at the back of the system case. This will allow the board's various sockets to be accessible from behind.

Establish which type of socket the board is designed for and then simply plug it in. Power up the PC and slip the driver CD into the CD-ROM drive. This should automatically load, presenting you with an install button. Click on this and you're away.

You will then be prompted to re-boot the PC. If it restarts as normal, displaying the usual diagnosis tests, then you know the card has been installed correctly.

The above procedure will be the same for whatever type of expansion card you decide to install. They will all come with a driver, either on a floppy disk or CD, usually the latter. Depending on what sort of application you are installing, you might then have to make or alter some settings to get the hardware running properly. Usually, thanks to Windows' plug and play feature, this is done for you.

Installing Hardware via Windows

Once you have fitted a new piece of hardware into your PC, the installation process may be over if you are using Plug and Play devices as just discussed (also see page 36–37). However, if Windows doesn't appear to have recognised the new hardware, you should try to let Windows acknowledge it via the Add New Hardware Wizard, or another device-specific Wizard. Select *Settings*, *Control Panel* from the Start menu. If you have just fitted a new modem, select the *Modems* icon – this will start the Install New Modem Wizard. Otherwise, select the *Add New Hardware* icon, and answer the questions that you are asked.

Troubleshooting

Having bought a brand new car most people, initially at least, like to look after it. They keep it nice and clean, have it regularly serviced and wouldn't dream of roaring along at 50mph in 3rd gear or driving it cross country. Given a new computer though and all such common sense seems to fly out of the window. They stick bits on it, shut it down when programs are running and expect it to do things that it just isn't capable of. Not surprisingly the computer goes wrong. The purpose of this chapter is to cover the main dos and don'ts and also to run through the more common problems people experience.

Covers

Chapter Seven

Introduction

As you will no doubt have discovered by now, your computer is a rare box of tricks and because of that fact it is rather prone to the odd anomaly. When you consider all the peripherals added to it you can see the potential for disaster. As has already been said however, most problems with PCs are caused by the user, either through ignorance or by refusing to follow a few basic dos and don'ts.

1   For example you must, whenever possible, shut the PC down properly. If you shut it down when data is being written or read you run the risk of corrupting your hard disk and Windows start up files. Then you will have all sorts of problems that could have been avoided.

2   When installing and uninstalling programs always use an uninstall program. This will ensure that the PC is returned to the state it was in prior to the program being installed.

3   Never, never plug anything into your PC while it's switched on unless you are using a USB port.

4   Make sure you are not asking your PC to do something that it is not capable of. For example don't expect it to play one of the lastest 3D games if it's only got 16 Mb of RAM and a 166Mhz CPU.

Just following these four rules alone will enable you to avoid many of the problems detailed in this chapter.

Windows

Problem   Windows doesn't start.

Cause   A floppy disk has been left inserted in the floppy disk drive. If this is the case you will see a message at the bottom of the screen saying – *invalid system disk*. Replace the disk and then press any key. What's happening here is that the PC is looking for the Windows Start Up files and the floppy drive is the first place it looks in. If the inserted floppy doesn't contain these files then the boot-up process will stop at this point.

Solution   Simply remove the floppy disk and press any key.

Cause   You see a message saying *General Protection Fault.* This happens when a serious system error has occurred, such as programs competing for the same resources thus causing a conflict.

Solution   You must re-boot the PC and if the error persists go into *Safe Mode*. This mode will start Windows with a minimal set of reliable drivers and allow you to find out what is stopping Windows from starting normally. To start in Safe Mode, restart the PC and hold down the CTRL key as it starts. Select Safe Mode from the options presented. Once back in Windows the best option is to follow the steps outlined in the Windows troubleshooter on *Startup and Shutdown.* This will be found under *Start, Help, Troubleshooting.*

Problem   Windows won't shut down.

Cause   The Windows exit sound file is damaged.

Solution   Go into *Control Panel, Sounds.* Under *Events* click *Exit Windows.* Under name click *None.* Restart the PC.

Cause   Windows *Fast Shutdown* feature is enabled. This feature is incompatible with some hardware devices and can cause PCs to stop responding.

Solution   To disable it go to *Run* and type *msconfig* in the box. Click ok. In the dialogue box that appears click *Advanced* and then select Disable *Fast Shutdown*. Restart the PC and then shut it down.

Cause   The Advanced Power Management feature is enabled. Under certain circumstances this can stop Windows from shutting down.

Solution   To disable it go into *Control Panel, System, Device Manager, System Devices, Settings, Advanced Power Management*. Click the clear *Enable Power Management* check box and restart the PC.

Problem   The computer locks up or freezes. This is due to a program crashing.

Solutions   To unfreeze the system try the following:

a)   Try switching to another Windows application by pressing Alt + Tab or Alt + Esc.

b)   Press Ctrl, Alt, Delete, which will bring up a Close Program dialog box. Try closing the offending program from here.

c)   If the program is really awkward then hit Ctrl, Alt, Delete again. This will perform a soft re-boot. Run the program again and if it is still misbehaving reinstall it.

Problem   When running the disk defragmenter the program keeps restarting.

Solutions   a)   Close any other applications that are open, interfering with the defragmenter. This includes any screensavers.

b)   Upgrade the system's RAM capability. A lack of system RAM means Windows has to write to the hard drive.

...cont'd

Problem   CDs autoplay when they are loaded into the CD-ROM drive.

Solutions   Disable Windows' CD autoplay feature.

a)   Go into *Control Panel, System, Device Manager,* click the + sign next to the CD-ROM, click your CD-ROM, select *settings* and remove the tick from *Auto Insert Notification.*

b)   Hold down the shift key when loading the CD until the drive light goes out.

This latter option is the better of the two as it leaves the feature activated for the next CD.

Problem   The PC seems to be running a lot slower than it used to.

Solutions   The System is becoming clogged up with redundant data.

a)   Empty the *Recycle Bin.*

b)   Empty the *Temporary Internet Files* folder.

c)   Empty the *Temp* folder.

d)   Purge the *Start Up* folder.

e)   Consider deleting any *Utility* programs you might have running as these can be a serious drain on the system's resources.

Problem   The Temporary Internet Files folder is full of something called *Cookies.*

Cause   Most Web sites you visit whilst browsing will download a small data file to your PC. This file or *Cookie,* as its known, is used the next time you visit that site. For example if the site in question requires a password before being accessed, the cookie will allow you to enter the site without entering your password every time.

Solution   To get rid of the ones you don't want simply delete them in the normal way. To prevent them being loaded to your hard drive at all, go into *Control Panel, Internet, Advanced.* Scroll down to *Disable All Cookie Use* and tick.

Problem　Programs that were ok now suddenly won't run at all.

Cause　Many programs use the same Windows files. When some of these programs are uninstalled they take one or more of these 'shared' files with them. Other programs which need these files will then not run. This problem is more noticeable with programs similar in nature.

Solution　The answer is to simply reinstall the program that caused the problem in the first place or to reinstall the affected programs.

Problem　Having installed Paint Shop Pro (PSP) and then uninstalled it, you are now unable to open image files on your PC.

Cause　This happens because PSP has altered the file associations of your image files to ones that it recognises. When PSP is uninstalled the PC is trying to load these images on to a program that no longer exists.

Solutions
a) Reinstall PSP. Your images will now open with PSP.

b) Reinstall your preferred graphics program. It should associate itself with all your graphics file formats just as PSP did.

c) Go into *View, Folder Options, File Types* and restore the original file associations yourself.

Problem　The Taskbar has disappeared.

Solutions
a) Disable the taskbar autohide feature. Go into *Start, Settings, Taskbar & Start Menu* and remove the tick from the *Auto Hide* box.

b) The taskbar has been dragged off the screen. You will see a thin line where it was – simply position the cursor on this line and drag it back into position.

...cont'd

Problem   My icons are damaged or mixed up.

     Solution   The easiest way round this is to install the *Tweak UI* program which you'll find on the Windows 98 CD under *Tools, Reskit, Powertoy*. Right click on the Tweak UI inf icon and then click *install*. The program will be installed in the Control Panel. Open the program, click the *repair* tab, then the *repair now* button. All your icons will be restored.

Display

Problem   The monitor screen is blank.

     Solutions
a)   Check all the monitor connections.

b)   Check the graphics card is seated correctly in the motherboard socket.

c)   Check the graphics card is ok by substituting it with another one or try the existing card in another system.

d)   Try the monitor on a different system.

e)   Replace the motherboard.

Problem   The monitor goes blank after a period of inactivity.

     Solutions
a)   Check if the 'none' option is selected under *screensavers* in *Display Properties.* Cancel it or increase the time delay period before it comes on.

b)   If your computer has an advanced power management system, it may be switching your PC to a *suspend* or *hibernate* state. Cancel it or increase the delay period.

Problem   The monitor is displaying garbled text.

     Solutions
a)   Try decreasing the hardware acceleration rate of the graphics card in *Control Panel, Display, Settings, Advanced, Performance.*

b)   Select a lower colour resolution in *Display Properties, Settings.*

...cont'd

Problem   The size of the displayed image is different than normal.

Solution   In *Display Properties, Settings* check that the *screen area* slider hasn't been inadvertently moved.

Problem   Faintly visible on the screen are two horizontal lines each about 6cm from the top and bottom edges.

Cause   This is a problem common to all monitors using Diamondtron CRTs made by Mitsubishi and Trinitron CRTs made by Sony. The lines are shadows from the damper wires which are an integral part of the internal structure of the monitor.

Solution   Unfortunately this problem is something the user has to learn to live with.

Memory

Problem   You receive an 'out of memory' message when starting or running a program.

Solutions
a) When you quit the previous program, it may not have returned the memory resources it was using to the system. Quit the current program, restart the computer and try the program again.

b) The program could be damaged, causing memory problems. Try reinstalling it.

c) Close any other programs you may have running as the system might be struggling to cope with them all.

d) Check in the *Startup* folder that you don't have too many programs starting automatically with Windows. If you do, try removing some of them.

e) Try emptying the recycle bin, temporary files, obsolete files and seldom used programs as there may not be enough hard disk space for the virtual memory file used by Windows to simulate RAM.

Disk Drive

Problem   Hard, CD-ROM or Floppy drives are not being recognised by the system.

Solutions

a)   There are loose cable connections. Make sure any plugs are firmly seated.

b)   Device drivers are missing or damaged. Reinstall them and then check in *Control Panel, System, Device Manager* that the driver is present.

c)   There is a hardware conflict. Reconfigure the offending device.

d)   A boot sector virus could have spread from an infected floppy disk to the hard disk and can prevent the disk controller drivers being loaded. Check with a suitable anti-virus program.

e)   The drive unit itself is faulty. Try substituting it with one you know to be working.

Problem   You are unable to access the Floppy disk drive.

Solutions

a)   The disk may not be formatted. You will get a message informing you of this. Format it by right clicking on the drive icon and choosing the *Format* option.

b)   The disk could be write protected. Remove the protection by sliding back the plastic tab located at the rear upper left hand corner of the disk.

c)   The read/write heads may be dirty. Clean them with a head cleaning kit available at most computer suppliers.

d)   Has the disk been compressed? If so it needs to be mounted before it can be accessed. This can be done in *System Tools, Drivespace*.

Problem   You are unable to access the CD-ROM drive.

    Solutions
a) Your CD might be dirty or damaged. Clean it by holding under running water and polishing it with a lint free cotton cloth. Do not use paper products.

b) The read/write heads could be dirty. Clean them with a proprietary cleaning CD.

c) The CD drive lens may be dirty. This can have all sorts of symptoms including the system freezing and crashing. A lens cleaning disk run through a few times will cure the problem.

Problem   Your hard disk drive is rapidly running out of space and you don't know why.

    Solutions
a) If you spend a lot of time browsing the web, a folder called *Temporary Internet Files* can very rapidly fill up with enormous amounts of data. Web browsers store information on the various sites you have visited in the form of *Cookies*, in order to quickly reload that page should you return to it. All this stuff can be safely ditched.

b) Have you checked the Recycle Bin recently? Many people merrily consign their data to the bin completely forgetting that it needs emptying occasionally to remove the data from the drive.

Modem

Problem   The modem is not recognised by the system.

Solutions
a) You may have poor connections, check them all.

b) The driver could be missing or damaged, reinstall it.

c) Is your modem properly configured? The preferred configuration is COM 2, IRQ 3. If your modem is using other resources it may not function.

d) Try a different modem.

Problem   Software reporting no dial tone.

Solutions
a) Check the telephone conection is ok and make sure that the telephone line is connected to the modem.

b) Check the telephone is connected to the correct jackplug on the modem.

c) Make sure any other devices connected to the same line, such as an answering machine, are off-hook.

Problem   The modem does not work at specified speed.

Solutions   For a modem to work at its maximum speed it must be operating under optimum conditions. However this is rarely, if ever, the case. You can however try the following:

a) Make sure there are no other devices connected to the line.

b) Remove any connectors, splitters or surge protectors. Line splitters for example will reduce the strength of the signal across the phone line. Your phone line should go directly from the modem to the phone socket.

c) Check that your Service Provider's modem supports the same data transmission speed that yours does.

d) As a last resort contact the phone company and ask them to check your line for noise.

Problem   Your Internet connection is periodically broken.

    Solutions   a)   There could be transients, i.e. power surges. Try fitting a surge protector.

                b)   There might be faults at the Service Provider's end. For example at certain times, the weekend especially, the system may be unable to cope with the volume of traffic. Try a different ISP.

Problem   Online connections occasionally 'pause' before picking up again.

    Cause   The usual reason for this is an overloaded system. As Internet usage increases this is becoming an ever increasing problem.

    Solution   The only solution is to try a different ISP or try to avoid peak periods.

Keyboard

Problem   You receive a keyboard error message when starting up your computer.

    Solution   Restart the PC. If a key is accidentally pressed during the booting process, an electrical circuit is broken. As a result the system will not recognise the keyboard and will say so.

Problem   The keyboard's response is too slow. This can be a problem to people who are skilled typists.

    Solution   Adjust how quickly a letter reaches the screen from the keyboard. Go into *Control Panel*, *Keyboard* and *Speed*. Under delay you can change the keyboard speed.

Problem   You are getting characters that don't correspond to the keyboard characters. A common example of this is # instead of £.

    Solution   Go into *Control Panel*, *Keyboard*, *Language* and make sure the language you want is selected.

Printer

Problem   The printer is completely dead, i.e. no lights on the control
panel.

Solutions   a)   Make sure the printer is switched on.

b)   Check that the printer cable is securely connected to
the correct sockets.

Problem   The power light is on but printer doesn't work.

Solutions   a)   Run a printer operation check as detailed in the
printer manual. This will involve removing the
interface cable and then pressing a combination of
the Control Panel buttons.

b)   If it still doesn't print then there is a fault with the
printer or its cable. Try a different cable and if that
doesn't help, refer back to the manufacturer.

c)   If the printer itself is ok, then it will print out a test
page. You now know the fault is software related.

d)   Make sure the printer and application software is
correctly installed. If in doubt re-install it.

e)   Go into the *spool manager* and check that there are no
stalled print jobs. If there are cancel them.

f)   Check that printing isn't *paused* in the printer
software.

g)   Check the printer is connected to the right port –
usually LPT1.

h)   Try printing from a different application.

i)   Check that the computer has enough memory to
handle the amount of data in the printer file.

Problem   The printer software indicates that the printer is offline.

Solution   In spool manager make sure the *Print Manager* box is
ticked.

...cont'd

Problem   The printer appears to be working but nothing is being printed.

   Solutions   a)   The print head nozzles are clogged. Clean the nozzles using the appropriate option in the printer software.

                      b)   The ink cartridge is empty. Replace it with a new one.

Problem   The printing quality is poor, i.e. faint, gaps in the text or white horizontal lines.

   Solutions   a)   Make sure the print head nozzles are not clogged.

                      b)   The printer settings could be incorrect, so make sure the media type setting chosen is appropriate for the paper being used.

                      c)   Deselect the high speed option in the printer settings.

Scanner

Problem   Operating the scanner causes the PC to crash.

Cause   This problem is usually caused by the interface cards often supplied with scanners. These cards can conflict with other cards or components in the PC thus causing the system to crash.

Solution   Use the *Device Manager* in *Control Panel, System* to isolate which device is conflicting with the scanner. Having done this the device must be reconfigured to eliminate the conflict.

Problem   The TWAIN software reports a TWAIN error.

Cause   TWAIN (technology without an interesting name) software is the interface between the scanner and the PC. What sometimes happens is that when new software is installed it overwrites files in the Windows system, one or more of which may be TWAIN files.

Solution   Reinstall the TWAIN software.

Problem   The scanned image does not contain all the information in the original.

Cause   The preview window in the scanner software has not been set correctly.

Solution   Resize it by dragging it so that it encloses the whole of the document to be scanned.

Problem   The scanned image takes a long time to be displayed on screen.

Solutions   a)   Decrease the scan resolution. Scanning at unnecessarily high resolutions can result in huge file sizes. The system will take a long time to open them.

b)   Increase your system's RAM. Processing image data is very memory intensive and if the main memory is unable to handle the size of the scan, then Windows has to take over by utilising part of the hard drive. This process can take a long time.

Games

Problem

Games don't run at all or you get a message saying something like 'your system doesn't have 3D acceleration'.

Solution

You will have to upgrade your existing graphics card. Many of today's games will not work at all without a 3D accelerator graphics card. (see pages 23–24)

Problem

Games run but not very well. For example they may be slow and jerky.

Solutions

a) Make sure your system is up to the game's requirements in terms of processing speed and memory capacity. Many games are resource intensive and will not work well on low specified systems. Typically you will need a minimum of a Pentium II or equivalent, with a good 3D graphics card and 32Mb of RAM.

b) Ensure that you have the latest drivers for the games. If not you need to install them.

c) Terminate all other running applications before running games. Other programs can interfere with the games operation as well as using up system resources needed by the game.

Problem

Games lock up or cause system crashes.

a) Close down other applications that are running at the same time.

b) The hardware acceleration is set too high. Try turning it down in *Control Panel, Display, Settings, Advanced, Performance.*

c) Try running the game at a lower screen resolution or with less colours.

d) Either free up space on your hard drive or increase your system's RAM.

Problem   How to exit a game when it has no exit feature.

      Solution   Perform a soft re-boot with *Ctrl, Alt, Del*. Before the system starts up again switch it off. The trick is to try and ensure there is no disk access – if you power down when the computer is writing data to the hard drive, it could corrupt it.

Maintenance

Although computers do not need much in the way of maintenance there are, however, certain things you ought to be aware of.

Heat   Electronic circuitry has an inherent potential to self-destruct and the seed of this tendency comes in the form of heat, specifically *excessive* heat. Fifty percent or more of the power given to an electronic chip, the CPU for example, will do nothing more productive than generate heat and if this is not safely dissipated, the chip will fry.

To this end PCs are provided with fans, usually two, one mounted on the outside of the CPU itself and another towards the rear of the case. When positioning your PC it is most important that you do nothing to obstruct the ventilation grille at the back. Another point worth mentioning here is that if you add a lot of expansion cards later on you will inevitably be creating even more heat, perhaps beyond the fan's extraction capabilities. Your computer manual will tell you at what temperature you can safely operate your PC and it might, in these circumstances, be worth checking it with a thermometer.

Dust   Dust, as we all know, is pervasive. It gets everywhere and over a period of time builds up on the inside of your PC covering the circuit boards in a layer of insulation. Periodically (once a year say) open up your PC and blow off any dust you see with a can of compressed air. Also make sure to clean the air circulation grille while you're at it.

Magnets

Magnets are a potential source of irritation bearing in mind that hard and floppy disk drives are electro-magnetic devices. Place a powerful magnet too close to a floppy disk containing important data and you may be more than just irritated. Remember that magnets can be found in devices such as speakers and monitors, although nowadays these are shielded, you should be aware of what can happen.

Power Surges

The socket that a PC is plugged into can cause transients, i.e. power surges. These can happen in two ways. The first is fluctuations in the mains supply – momentary increases in the supply voltage which usually will have little effect on your PC other than to cause the occasional crash or lost Internet connection. Severe surges, such as those caused by lightening, can cook your PC completely, so always unplug your computer when the dog starts shaking and dives behind the sofa. Remember also to remove the aerial if you have a TV tuner card. Powering up also causes voltage surges. Every time you switch on your PC, or indeed any electrical device, it will for a split second be drawing several times more power than normal and it won't like it. When do light bulbs blow? Often when they're switched on.

The solutions to this problem are simple. Firstly, voltage smoothing devices are available which will keep the supply to the PC stable and 'spike' free. Secondly, consider leaving your PC on all the time. The cost of this is negligible as the most power hungry component, the monitor, can be switched off. Alternatively, many systems have standby or suspend modes the same as a TV, where the monitor and hard drive are powered down after a set period.

Electrostatic Electricity

Electrostatic electricity is an electric charge, which can be built up in the human body by, for example, walking across a nylon carpet. When you then touch something conductive such as metal, the voltage discharges giving you a tingle. While electrostatic electricity is minute in terms of current, the voltage can be enormous and electronic components, chips especially, will not be pleased if subjected to it. So if for any reason you delve inside your PC, you *must* earth yourself by touching something metal, the PC case will do.

Index